EDUCATIONAL ACHIEVEMENT IN JAPAN

LYNEAZJ.98

Educational Achievement in Japan

Lessons for the West

Richard Lynn
Professor of Psychology
University of Ulster

M.E. SHARPE, INC.
ARMONK, NEW YORK

First published in Great Britain by the Macmillan Press Ltd.

Published in 1988 in the United States by M. E. Sharpe, Inc.
80 Business Park Drive, Armonk, New York 10504

Printed in Great Britain

Library of Congress Cataloging-in-Publication Data
Lynn, Richard.
Educational achievement in Japan.
Bibliography: p.
Includes index.
1. Educational—Japan.   2. Academic achievement.
I. Title.
LA1312.L96   1988   370′.952   87–28377
ISBN 0–87332–469–2 (pbk.)

To the memory of Esmée Fairbairn

Contents

List of Tables   xi

1 Introduction   **1**

2 Educational Standards in Japan   **4**

   2.1   The First International Study of Achievement in
            Mathematics   4
   2.2   The International Study of Science Achievement   9
   2.3   The Sendai-Minneapolis-Taipei Study   11
   2.4   The Illinois-Japan Study of Mathematics   14
   2.5   The Second International Study of Achievement
            in Mathematics   15
   2.6   Age Trends in Japanese Educational Standards   16
   2.7   Conclusions   17

3 The Japanese School System   **18**

   3.1   Kindergarten   18
   3.2   Primary Schools   20
   3.3   The Curriculum   21
   3.4   Junior High Schools   22
   3.5   Supplementary Education: the Juku   23
   3.6   Senior High Schools   26
   3.7   Public and Private Senior High Schools   30
   3.8   The Rise of the Private Senior High Schools   33
   3.9   Japan's Leading Senior High School: Nada   36
   3.10 Contemporary Standing of Public and Private
            Senior High Schools   38
   3.11 State Subsidies to Private Schools   39
   3.12 Vocational High Schools and Technical Colleges   41
   3.13 Universities   42
   3.14 Conclusions   47

4 The Intelligence of Japanese Children   **52**

   4.1   Intelligence and Educational Achievement   52

4.2	Non-Verbal Tests of Japanese Intelligence	52
4.3	The Pattern of Japanese Abilities	54
4.4	Contribution of Japanese Intelligence to Educational Achievement	58
4.5	Conclusions	60

5 Motivation and Incentives for Educational Achievement in Japan and the West — **61**

5.1	Incentives and Educational Achievement	62
5.2	Motivation of Japanese School Children	64
5.3	Incentives in Japanese Education	65
5.4	Three Parameters of Incentives for Work Motivation	67
5.5	Marks and Grades as Incentives	70
5.6	The Incentive Function of Selection for Secondary Schools in Britain, the United States and Continental Europe	71
5.7	Public Examinations as Incentives in Britain	73
5.8	Minimum Competence Tests as Incentives in the United States	74
5.9	Incentives for Mastery of an Academic Curriculum	75
5.10	Co-operation and Competition in Schools	76
5.11	Conclusions	78

6 The Intrinsic Motivation of Japanese School Children — **80**

6.1	Four Types of Intrinsic Work Motivation	80
6.2	The Development of Intrinsic Motivation	83
6.3	Intrinsic Motivation in Japanese Children	85
6.4	The Role of Parents in the Acquisition of Intrinsic Motivation	87
6.5	Complementary Relationship between Extrinsic and Intrinsic Motivation	90
6.6	Conclusions	92

7 The Contribution of Teachers and Schools to Educational Achievement — **94**

7.1	The Professionalism of Japanese Teachers	94
7.2	Government Specification of the Curriculum	96

7.3	Competition Between Schools	99
7.4	Private Schools	102
7.5	Teachers' Abilities	103
7.6	Teachers' Training and Qualifications	105
7.7	Teachers' Remuneration	106
7.8	Financial Resources for Schools	108
7.9	Teacher-Pupil Ratios and the Size of Classes	110
7.10	Instruction Time: School Work and Homework	113
7.11	Conclusions	119
8	**Four Lessons for the West**	**121**
8.1	Incentives for School Children	121
8.2	Some Possible Costs of the Japanese System	125
8.3	Length of the School Year	128
8.4	Incentives for Teacher Efficiency	129
8.5	Government Specification of the Curriculum	132
8.6	Competition Between Schools	136
8.7	The Privatisation of Schools	138
8.8	Conclusions	142
References		145
Name Index		152
Subject Index		155

List of Tables

2.1 Means and standard deviations for 13-year-olds in mathematics   5

2.2 Mean scores of 18-year-old mathematics specialists and non-specialists   7

2.3 Science achievement of 10- and 14-year-olds in 13 countries   10

2.4 Achievement scores in mathematics, reading vocabulary and reading comprehension   13

2.5 Japanese–American differences in mathematics in 1981   14

2.6 Percentage correct scores of 13-year-olds on 18 mathematics tests, calculated from the second international study of achievement in mathematics   16

2.7 Japanese–United States disparities in maths and science shown in relation to age of children   17

4.1 Mean IQs of Japanese children in relation to white American means of 100 and standard deviation of 15   56

6.1 Mean scores on attitude to school work questionnaires of 13- and 18-year-olds (mathematics) and 10- and 14-year-olds (science)   86

6.2 Comparison of mothers' attitudes to children's abilities and the effectiveness of schools in Japan, the United States and Taiwan   89

7.1 Teachers' estimates of coverage of the curriculum for 13-year-olds in maths and 14-year-olds in science   98

7.2 Abilities of teachers at primary and secondary schools   104

7.3 Length of tertiary education of primary and secondary school teachers   105

7.4 Indices of teachers' pay in 13 countries   106

7.5 Correlations between indices of teachers' pay and children's science attainment scores   107

7.6 Expenditure per pupil in US dollars for 13-year-olds, 18-year-old mathematician specialists and 18-year-old non-mathematicians   109

7.7 Public expenditure as a percentage of gross national product (GNP) in the 18 economically advanced western nations for the year 1980   110

7.8   Class sizes and teacher-pupil ratios in various
      countries   112
7.9   Various measures of time devoted to school work in
      different countries   115
7.10 Time spent on mathematics, given as percentages of
      total instruction time, as hours per annum and as
      minutes per week homework   118
8.1   Proportions of students studying science and
      engineering in 1970   127

1 Introduction

The objective of this book is to present an account of the education system in Japan for the interest and, hopefully, for the benefit of educationists, social scientists and politicians in Britain, the United States and Continental Europe. In the West, educational standards have in recent decades become an increasing cause of public concern. In Japan, educational standards are exceptionally high, such that by adolescence average Japanese teenagers are some three years ahead of their counterparts in the West. It is therefore in an attempt to analyse how the high educational standards in Japan are achieved, and what lessons the West might usefully learn from the Japanese school system, that this book has been written.

In Britain a growing sense of public disquiet about education can be dated from the late 1960s. In 1969 there appeared the first of the series of Black Papers and similar publications on education, written by a group who were critical of what they considered to be unacceptably poor educational standards and of the increasing influence of undemanding new philosophies in education, and who wished to reassert the importance of traditional academic values (Cox and Dyson, 1969; Boyson, 1972). It was not only among the more traditionally minded that these concerns were expressed. It was the Labour prime minister, Mr James Callaghan, who in 1976 called for a national debate on educational standards and the problem of how they could be raised.

In the 1970s two government commissions were set up to consider the question of educational standards in British schools and make appropriate recommendations. In 1975 the Bullock Report documented the existence of a disconcertingly high proportion of school leavers who were illiterate or semi-illiterate and proposed various remedies; and in 1982 the Cockcroft Report did a similar job for mathematics, in which it documented the high proportion, amounting to approximately one third of the population, who were unable to do simple mental arithmetic (Bullock, 1975; Cockcroft, 1982). There have been many complaints in Britain that educational standards have actually been declining, but there is no adequate research for any definitive judgement on this question. But whether or not educational standards have been declining, there is virtually universal agreement that educational standards are not high enough for employment and

1

citizenship in an advanced technological society. The high rates of unemployment which have been present in Britain during the 1980s, as in most other advanced Western economies, have been largely confined to those with poor educational skills and qualifications. Among many skilled occupations there has remained a shortage of labour rather than a shortage of jobs. This is one of the reasons, although not the only one, why it is widely felt that educational standards need to be raised.

Public concern over educational standards has been even greater in the United States than in Britain. There is clear evidence that literacy and numeracy among school leavers have fallen in the United States since the mid-1960s. This evidence is partly derived from the scores achieved each year by hundreds of thousands of American adolescents in the Scholastic Aptitude Test, which is largely a test of verbal comprehension, reading and mathematics. Studies made by the National Assessment of Educational Progress have also documented a decline in educational standards in the United States. These studies have shown that in the mid-1970s approximately 20 per cent of American 18-year-olds have been illiterate and around 60 per cent semi-illiterate. A detailed review of the evidence on declining standards in the United States has been given by Lerner (1983).

By the early 1980s the United States government had become alarmed by the mounting evidence of widespread illiteracy, innumeracy and falling standards among school leavers. A National Commission on Excellence in Education was established and reported in 1983 in a paper entitled *A Nation at Risk*. This paper documented in detail the extent of the problem and the decline in standards which had taken place since 1963. The report went so far as to declare that 'if an unfriendly foreign power had attempted to impose on America the mediocre educational performance that exists today, we might have well viewed it as an act of war. As it stands, we have allowed this to happen to ourselves'. The American public has reacted to the declining standards of the public schools by a flight into private education. The number of children in private schools grew by 66 per cent during the 1970s (Boyer, 1983). So strong has dissatisfaction with the public schools become that many parents, according to two educationists, have been 'frantically seeking alternatives to public education' (Donovan and Madaus, 1985, p. 52).

There are no problems of this kind in Japan. In so far as there is public concern about education in Japan, it is rather that education is too competitive and that school children are working too hard at the expense of their social and cultural development. To the Western observer these are to some degree enviable problems and certainly they raise the question of how this dedication to school work in Japan is achieved and whether the West can profit from the Japanese example.

In attempting to answer this question we proceed in the following stages. First, in Chapter 2 the evidence on educational standards in Japan and the extent of the lead of Japanese children over those in the economically advanced nations of the West is set out in detail. Chapter 3 presents a largely descriptive account of the educational system in Japan to acquaint the reader with the broad outline of the way the system works. In Chapter 4 we begin an analysis of the factors responsible for the high educational standards in Japan. We follow Parkerson, Schiller, Lomax and Walberg (1984) in adopting for the problem of educational achievement the approach of the production models constructed by economists. In these output is conceptualised as the product of a variety of factors such as capital investment, the costs of raw materials, the availability of skilled labour, entrepreneurial ability and so forth, and the relative contributions of these can be quantified. Similarly, the educational standards of children can usefully be conceptualised as an output, the principal determinants of which are the intelligence and motivation of children, the attitudes of parents, the motivation and professionalism of teachers, the time devoted to learning and the financial resources available to schools. The contributions of these to Japanese educational standards are discussed in successive chapters. It is seen that in a number of these respects Japanese school children enjoy advantages over those in the West and an analysis is offered of how these advantages are secured.

In the final chapter we consider what practical steps could be taken to introduce into the education systems of the West some of the features responsible for the high educational standards of Japanese school children. Thus we conclude with an attempt to provide answers to the problem with which we started, namely what lessons can usefully be learned in Britain, the United States and other nations of the West from the way in which such high educational standards are achieved in Japan.

2 Educational Standards in Japan

In this chapter we set out the evidence on educational standards in Japan compared with those in the economically advanced nations of the West. In making comparisons of this kind the range of academic subjects for which comparisons can be made is necessarily restricted, because for many subjects different curricula are taught in different countries. For instance, school children learn principally the literature and history of their own countries and there is no meaningful way in which, for instance, Japanese children's knowledge of the literature and history of Japan can be compared with British children's knowledge of the literature and history of Britain. International comparisons of educational standards therefore have to be confined to mathematics, science and reading, where the curriculum is at least broadly the same in all economically advanced nations.

2.1 THE FIRST INTERNATIONAL STUDY OF ACHIEVEMENT IN MATHEMATICS

The first study to reveal the high educational standards in Japan was the international study of achievement in mathematics carried out in the mid-1960s (Husen, 1967). In this investigation data were collected from 12 countries regarding achievement in mathematics of 13-year-olds and 18-year-olds. Mathematics tests were administered to representative samples of around two or three thousand 13-year-olds and several hundred 18-year-olds (the numbers tested varying somewhat between countries). In addition, a considerable amount of further information was collected concerning schools, teachers and pupil attitudes, from which is was possible to estimate the effects of these on pupils' performance. In spite of being some 20 years old now, the study remains a mine of useful and interesting information and analysis.

For the 13-year-olds two sets of results were given. The first consisted of mean scores of the samples of all 13-year-olds from the various countries and the second of samples from the standard school grade where most 13-year-olds were placed. (Thus, for example, in

England and the USA most 13-year-olds are in the second year of secondary school and the grade figure would be for these.) The grade data include unknown numbers of 12-year-olds, 13-year-olds and 14-year-olds. It would seem that the first of these two sets of data is the more satisfactory, since it is better to compare the educational attainments of children of a given age. Nevertheless, the two sets of results correspond fairly closely as can be seen in Table 2.1, where the data are displayed.

Table 2.1   Means and standard deviations for 13-year-olds in mathematics

Country	13-year-olds		Standard grade for 13-year-olds	
	Mean	S.D.	Mean	S.D.
Australia	20.2	14.0	18.9	12.3
Belgium	27.7	15.0	30.4	13.7
England	19.3	17.0	23.8	18.5
Finland	–	–	–	–
France	18.3	12.4	21.0	13.2
Germany	–	–	25.4	11.7
Israel	–	–	32.3	14.7
Japan	31.2	16.9	31.2	16.9
Netherlands	23.9	15.9	21.4	12.1
Scotland	19.1	14.6	22.3	15.7
Sweden	15.7	10.8	15.3	10.8
United States	16.2	13.3	17.8	13.3
Total	19.8	14.9	23.0	15.0

Source: Husen (1967)

The mean scores show quite a wide range between countries. It will be seen that Japanese children achieved the highest mean in the first sample (all 13-year-olds) and the second highest in the second sample (the typical 13-year-old grade). In the second sample the highest mean was obtained by the Israeli children and, for some reason not explained by the investigators, an Israeli mean for the first sample was not calculated. For the second sample the Israeli children were six months older than the Japanese children which precludes comparison between the two samples.

The most satisfactory method of estimating the magnitude of the Japanese children's lead over those in other countries is to calculate the difference between the means in standard deviation units. Thus, in the case of the Japanese and English children the mean scores are 31.2 and 19.3 respectively, a difference of 11.9 points. The standard deviation (SD) for the entire set of nations is 14.9, so that the Japanese children scored higher than the English by 0.80 per cent of a standard deviation. This means that approximately 79 per cent of Japanese children obtained a higher score than the average English child. In comparison with children in the United States, Japanese children's scores were higher by 15 points or almost exactly 1 standard deviation. This meant that approximately 84 per cent of Japanese children scored higher than the average American child.

The second age group tested in this investigation was 18-year-olds in their last year of school. It should be noted that it is considerably more difficult to make valid cross-national comparisons with adolescents at this stage of their education. There are two particular problems here. First, there are considerable national differences in the proportions of adolescents who remain in school at the age of 18. In some countries well over half the age group were in school, whereas in others the proportion was around 10 per cent. A second problem with cross-national comparisons at this stage concerns the different extent to which students specialise in different countries. For instance, in England there is an unusually high degree of specialisation and therefore higher standards of attainment among maths specialists would be expected. Conversely, it might be expected that there should also be lower standards among arts specialists who have given up maths at the age of sixteen, while students in countries following a broader curriculum will have kept up their maths.

The investigators were aware of these problems and did their best to overcome them. First they divided the 18-year-olds into maths specialists and non-specialists. Secondly, they presented two sets of mean mathematics scores. The first set comprised the means of the total samples tested. The second set consisted of the means of the top 4 per cent of the age cohorts for the maths specialists and the top 3 per cent for the non-specialists. The second set of data simply discards the poorer students from the countries where large proportions of 18-year-olds remain at school and endeavours to compare like with like. This treatment is probably the best that can be done with the data. It goes some way towards meeting the problem of different proportions of 18-year-olds remaining at school in different countries, but it does not handle so well the problem of different degrees of specialisation which is probably insoluble. Nevertheless the data are well worth consideration and are shown in Table 2.2.

Table 2.2 Mean scores of 18-year-old mathematics specialists and non-specialists

Country	Percentage 18-year-olds in school	Number of subjects studied	All maths students		All non-maths students		Top 4% maths students		Top 3% of non-maths students	
			Mean	S.D.	Mean	S.D.	Mean	S.D.	Mean	S.D.
Australia	23	6	21.6	10.5	–	–	33.7	6.6	–	–
Belgium	13	9+	34.6	12.6	24.2	9.5	34.6	12.6	34.9	4.3
England	12	3	35.2	12.6	21.4	10.0	39.4	9.8	30.2	6.0
Finland	14	9	25.3	9.6	22.5	8.3	32.1	6.5	29.9	5.6
France	11	9+	33.4	10.8	–	–	37.0	8.0	–	–
W. Germany	11	9	28.8	9.8	27.7	7.6	31.5	7.8	34.2	4.0
Israel	–	8	36.4	8.6	–	–	41.7	4.4	–	–
Japan	57	9+	31.4	14.8	25.3	14.3	43.9	7.7	51.7	2.2
Netherlands	8	9+	31.9	8.1	–	–	34.7	6.2	–	–
Scotland	18	4	25.5	10.4	20.7	9.5	29.4	9.8	32.7	4.1
Sweden	23	9	27.3	11.9	12.6	6.2	43.7	6.2	21.8	3.8
United States	70	4	13.8	12.6	8.3	9.1	33.0	8.9	30.7	3.6

Source: Husen (1967)

This table gives figures for the nations for the percentage of 18-year-olds in school, the number of subjects typically studied by the 18-year-olds, and mean scores for the mathematics specialists and non-specialists of the total samples and of the top 4 per cent (maths specialists) and 3 per cent (non-specialists). It will be seen that there are considerable national variations in the proportions of 18-year-olds in school. In the United States 70 per cent were in school and in Japan 57 per cent, while in England, Germany, France and The Netherlands the proportions were only in the range of 8 to 12 per cent. Clearly it would not be reasonable to expect average educational standards to be as high in countries where over half the age group are in full-time education (the United States and Japan) as in other countries where only a small élite remain at school. This must be the main reason why the mean score of the total sample from the United States is so much lower than that of the other countries (approximately 1 standard deviation below the average). If we look at the second set of data (for the top 4 per cent of mathematics specialists and the top 3 per cent of non-specialists), it can be seen that the United States scores are greatly improved and fall broadly into line with those in other advanced Western countries.

Our main focus of interest is on Japan. If we look at the first set of means the most striking feature of the results is that the Japanese students do so well in spite of having an exceptionally high proportion of the age cohort in school. Both Japanese mathematics specialists and non-specialists obtain mean scores substantially above the average of the entire set of nations. The chief significance of these results is that in Japan over half the age cohort achieves broadly the same standards as small intellectual élites of around 10 to 20 per cent of the age group in other advanced Western countries.

The second set of mean scores (the top 4 per cent of mathematics specialists and top 3 per cent of non-specialists) is more meaningful because it equates for the different proportions of the cohort remaining in school in the different countries. If these means are examined, it will be seen that for both maths specialists and non-specialists the Japanese achieved the highest mean scores. Compared with England, the Japanese obtain a mean of 43.9 as against 39.4, a difference of 3.9 points which amounts to approximately a half standard deviation. It has to be borne in mind that the English students enjoyed an advantage by virtue of their greater specialisation in mathematics. The English 18-year-olds maths specialists would typically have been studying perhaps only three or four subjects for two years (ages sixteen to eighteen), and two of these subjects would typically have been pure and applied mathematics. On the other hand, the Japanese would have been carrying nine subjects for their university entrance examinations, which are set on a broader range of subjects, including both mathematics and English. Thus the superior achievement of the Japanese students has to be seen in the light of their handicap of having to follow a broader curriculum.

The same consideration applies to a comparison of the Japanese students with those of the United States, where the curriculum for mathematics specialists is also narrower than in Japan, consisting typically of four principal subjects. The mean scores of the Japanese and American students are 43.9 and 33.0 respectively. This difference of 10.9 points has to be considered in relation to a standard deviation of approximately 8, and means that among this group of mathematics specialists the average Japanese student does better than around 90 per cent of the corresponding American students.

Turning now to the 18-year-old non-specialists, the results in Table 2.2 again show that the Japanese achieved the best average result. The Japanese superiority here is very striking. The Japanese average is 3 to 4 standard deviations above that in the other countries and this means that the average Japanese student scores at about the same level as the top 1 per cent elsewhere. Of course these Japanese non-mathematicians would have had an advantage over 18-year-olds in England and the United States because they would have been keeping up some mathematics in the wider curriculum followed in Japanese schools, whereas most English and American non-mathematicians at the age of 18 would have given up their maths from the age of 16. But this would not explain the Japanese superiority in relation to most of the other countries where a broad curriculum in which most 18-year-olds continue to take some mathematics is the norm.

2.2 THE INTERNATIONAL STUDY OF SCIENCE ACHIEVEMENT

A broadly similar study to the international study of achievement in mathematics was carried out for science in 1970–1971 (Comber and Keeves, 1973). Eighteen countries participated in this investigation. These comprised the twelve countries in the mathematics study with the exception of Israel and with the addition of Hungary, Italy, New Zealand, Chile, India, Iran and Thailand.

Children were tested at the age of 10 and 14 years (and also at the age of 18, but the Japanese did not participate in this part of the study and it is therefore not considered here). The tests covered physics, biology, chemistry and earth sciences. The tests assessed knowledge of scientific facts; comprehension and ability to apply scientific information in new contexts; and higher processes involving the ability to formulate and solve problems by the experimental method. Between 1000–4000 children at each of the two ages were tested in each country, sampled as representative children from a large number of schools.

Table 2.3   Science achievement of 10- and 14-year-olds in 13 countries

Country	10-year-olds		14-year-olds	
	Mean	S.D.	Mean	S.D.
Australia	—	—	24.6	13.4
Belgium (Fl)	17.9	7.3	21.2	9.2
Belgium (Fr)	13.9	7.1	15.4	8.8
England	15.7	8.5	21.3	14.1
Finland	17.5	8.2	20.5	10.6
Germany (FR)	14.9	7.4	23.7	11.5
Hungary	16.7	8.0	29.1	12.7
Italy	16.5	8.6	18.5	10.2
Japan	21.7	7.7	31.2	14.8
Netherlands	15.3	7.6	17.8	12.9
New Zealand	—	—	24.2	12.9
Scotland	14.0	8.4	21.4	14.2
Sweden	18.3	7.3	21.7	11.7
United States	17.7	9.3	21.6	11.6
Mean	16.7	7.9	22.3	11.8

Source: Comber and Keeves (1973)

The details of the results for the advanced nations are shown in Table 2.3. The children from the four developing nations of India, Thailand, Chile and Iran obtained scores well below those of the advanced nations and are not shown here. Most notable from the point of view of our particular focus on Japan are the results that among both the 10-year-olds and the 14-year-olds the highest average scores were obtained by the Japanese children.

Looking first at the 10-year-olds, it can be seen that the Japanese children scored well above those from all other countries. All the other economically advanced countries obtained scores between 13.9 and 18.3, a fairly narrow range of 4.4 points. The Japanese mean of 21.7 is 3.4 points ahead of the next highest scoring country (Sweden). In standard deviation units, the Japanese children's mean score was 76 per cent of a standard deviation above the English children, and 51 per cent of a standard deviation above the American children (based on the standard deviation of the entire set of advanced nations). The high standard achieved by Japanese 10-year-olds was repeated among the 14-year-olds. Again the Japanese obtained the highest average score. Their average score of 31.2 is followed quite closely by Hungary at 29.1, but after this there is a considerable gap with most of the countries bunched in the narrow range between 20 and 25. At this age level, the Japanese scored 9.9 points above the English and 9.6 points above the Americans, representing in standard deviation units a lead of 84 per cent and 81 per cent respectively (based again on the entire set of economically advanced nations).

Thus both among 10-year-olds and 14-year-olds the Japanese children achieved the highest average scores. Furthermore, detailed breakdown of the scores showed that while the Japanese did well on tests requiring factual information, they did even better on tests requiring comprehension and higher processes involving application of scientific principles. These details are not given here and the interested reader is referred to the original publication, but it is worth noting that this result confounds the criticism sometimes made of Japanese education, to the effect that it stresses rote memorisation at the expense of higher mental processes involving the understanding and application of principles.

2.3 THE SENDAI–MINNEAPOLIS–TAIPEI STUDY

This investigation compared educational standards in reading and mathematics in Japan, the United States and in Taiwan. It was carried out in the late 1970s by a team in these three countries (Stigler, Lee, Lucker and Stevenson, 1982). Among the aims of the study was the collection of further evidence on Japanese educational standards by examining these at younger age levels, namely among 6 and 10-year-olds, to test for Japanese standards in reading in addition to mathematics, and finally to compare Japanese and American children (and Taiwanese) on a set of intelligence tests in order to determine how far the high standards of Japanese educational achievement could be explained in terms of high levels of intelligence. In all three countries compulsory education begins at the age of six and hence the first sample was young children of this age during their first year at school.

The children selected for the investigation were carefully drawn samples of 240 6-year-olds and 240 10-year-olds from each of the cities of Sendai in Japan, Minneapolis in the United States and Taipei in Taiwan. These cities were chosen as representing typical large cities with only very small minority populations in the respective countries. For the mathematics and reading tests considerable trouble was taken to examine the syllabus taught in the three countries and to construct tests which were equally fair for the children in terms of what they had been taught. In the case of mathematics the study showed that the Japanese curriculum introduced more mathematical concepts and skills even for 6-year-olds than was the case in either the United States or Taiwan.

The results of this investigation are summarised in Table 2.4. For the 6-year-olds only the mathematics test was given and the results showed that both the Japanese and Taiwanese children obtained higher average mean scores than those in the United States. These differences are statistically significant, but the slightly higher mean obtained by the Taiwan children compared with those in Japan is not significant. Combining the boys and girls, the Japanese mean is higher than the American by 3.2 points, representing 0.60 per cent of the American standard deviation, and therefore indicates that approximately 73 per cent of Japanese 6-year-olds obtain higher scores than the average American child.

The results for the 10-year-olds show that at this age the Japanese children were well ahead of both the Taiwanese and the Americans. The detailed figures given in Table 2.4 show that differences between the countries are substantial (all differences are statistically significant). Combining the scores of the boys and girls, the Japanese mean exceeds the American by 8.8 points. This represents 1.40 per cent of the American standard deviation and indicates that approximately 92 per cent of Japanese children obtained higher scores than the average American child among 10-year-olds. Thus the Japanese-American disparity has widened considerably between the ages of six and ten. The disparity has increased from 0.60 to 1.40 standard deviations, so that the Japanese lead has more than doubled during these years.

For the investigation of reading standards in the three countries only the 10-year-olds were used. Two measures of reading were given. These were (a) vocabulary, the ability to sight read single words; and (b) reading comprehension, the ability to read meaningful sentences and paragraphs and to respond to true-false and multiple-choice questions on them. The results shows little differences in the mean

Table 2.4 Achievement scores in mathematics, reading vocabulary and reading comprehension

| Country | Mathematics | | | | Vocabulary | | Comprehension | |
| | Boys | | Girls | | | | | |
	Mean	S.D.	Mean	S.D.	Mean	S.D.	Mean	S.D.
6-year-olds								
Japan	20.7	5.7	19.5	4.6				
Taiwan	21.2	5.4	21.1	5.6				
United States	16.6	5.5	17.6	5.2				
10-year-olds								
Japan	53.0	7.5	53.5	7.5	44.5	2.7	82.6	5.0
Taiwan	50.5	6.4	51.0	4.9	48.2	1.1	86.1	1.0
United States	45.0	6.5	43.8	5.9	46.2	4.2	84.5	4.0

Source: Stigler *et al.* (1982)

scores between the three countries. The Japanese children were in fact inferior on both tests; the difference is statistically significant for the vocabulary test but not for the comprehension. Nor were there any significant differences in the proportions of backward readers in the three countries.

In a further analysis of the data obtained in this study the mathematics scores of the children from the individual schools are given (Stevenson, 1983). These show that among 10-year-olds children in the school with the lowest score in Sendai were achieving higher means than those from the school with the highest score in Minneapolis. The interest of this result is that it shows how the whole range of ability in Japan is elevated above that in the United States.

2.4 THE ILLINOIS–JAPAN STUDY OF MATHEMATICS

This investigation of Japanese–American differences in educational achievement in mathematics was carried out in 1981 by Walberg, Harnisch and Tsai (1984). The samples tested were 15, 16 and 17-year-olds and consisted in the United States of approximately 9500 students in high schools throughout the state of Illinois, and in Japan of 1700 students drawn as a nationally representative sample. The test used was the American High School Mathematics Test which covers algebra, geometry, modern mathematics and probability.

Table 2.5   Japanese–American differences in mathematics in 1981

	Age			Sex	
	15	16	17	Boys	Girls
Japan mean	34.35	40.73	42.58	42.08	36.17
S.D.	6.79	8.91	9.34	9.37	7.73
United States mean	16.72	20.49	·15.87	19.88	19.32
S.D.	7.72	9.22	7.34	9.55	8.54

Source: Walberg, Harnisch and Tsai (1984)

The results of this study are shown in Table 2.5. Comparison of the average scores achieved in the United States and Japan shows the Japanese considerably ahead. The·Japanese lead amounts to more than two standard deviations, which means that the average Japanese performed better than around 98 per cent of American high school students. The American–Japanese disparity is broadly consistent at all of the three ages. Given also in this table are the scores achieved by boys and girls in the two countries. These show that boys score substantially higher than girls in Japan, while there is virtually no sex difference in the United States. The most probable explanation for this is that in Japan there is greater pressue on boys to achieve. There is little public expectation that Japanese girls will pursue high level professional careers, but rather than they will become wives and mothers or work in low status occupations. Nevertheless, Japanese girls score on average considerably higher than Americans of either sex.

2.5 THE SECOND INTERNATIONAL STUDY OF ACHIEVEMENT IN MATHEMATICS

During the early 1980s a second international study of achievement in mathematics was carried out on the same broad lines as the first study of the early 1960s. At the time of writing the results of this second study have not been fully analysed or published. However, preliminary results are available. These have been kindly supplied by Dr R. A. Garden, and will be summarised here.

Fourteen economically advanced nations took part in this study. The children tested consisted of well drawn representative samples of 13-year-olds and also of 18-year-olds. However, there are considerable difficulties in making cross-cultural comparisons with 18-year-olds, as noted above, because of the different proportions of this age group who remain in school in various countries, and the different degrees of specialisation in the curriculum followed. Statistical techniques have to be employed to overcome these problems and these have not yet been worked out. The results for the 18-year-olds will therefore not be pursued.

In the case of the 13-year-olds, 18 tests of various branches of mathematics were administered and the results for the children from the different countries given as percentages. These percentages have been averaged and these overall averages are shown in Table 2.6.

It is not possible to give the differences between the national means in standard deviation units, but once again it will be noted that the Japanese children come out well ahead of those in the other advanced nations.

Table 2.6   Percentage correct scores of 13-year-olds on 18 mathematics tests, calculated from the second international study of achievement in mathematics

Country	Score	Country	Score
Belgium	55.86	Japan	64.57
Canada	52.90	Luxembourg	40.98
England	48.61	Netherlands	59.07
Finland	49.40	New Zealand	46.91
France	57.18	Scotland	49.67
Hong Kong	51.33	Sweden	43.95
Hungary	58.40	USA	47.30

Source: unpublished data from second international study of achievement in mathematics

2.6 AGE TRENDS IN JAPANESE EDUCATIONAL STANDARDS

In the previous sections we have reviewed the results of eight samples of Japanese children and their educational standards. In all eight the Japanese children achieve higher standards in maths and science than those of children in Britain, the United States and other advanced Western nations. It is interesting to consider the Japanese lead in terms of the age of the children. To do this the results have been set out in relation to age and are shown in this way in Table 2.7. It is clear that the Japanese lead increases throughout the years of childhood and adolescence. It is smallest among 6-year-olds, although even here the Japanese lead is appreciable. But by the ages of 16 to 18 the Japanese lead has increased at least threefold.

The most straightforward way to interpret this age trend is in terms of the concept of cumulative advantage. This concept implies that any advantageous factors operating constantly over a period of years generates cumulative beneficial effects. The reason for this is that the initial educational and cognitive gains of year one become the foundation on which additional gains can be built in year two, and these in turn become the foundation for further gains in subsequent years. Thus the educational and cognitive skills develop cumulatively, in the same manner as the growth of a sum of money on deposit at a compound rate of interest. The concept of cumulative advantage has

Table 2.7 Japanese–United States disparities in attainment in maths and science shown in relation to age of children

Age	Japanese mean	US mean	US S.D.	Japanese lead in S.D.	Subject	Author
6	20.1	17.1	5.4	0.74	Maths	Stigler (1982)
10	21.7	12.7	9.3	0.97	Science	Comber (1973)
10	53.2	44.4	6.2	1.42	Maths	Stigler (1982)
13	31.2	16.2	13.3	1.13	Maths	Husen (1967)
14	31.2	21.6	11.6	0.83	Science	Comber (1973)
16	40.73	20.49	9.22	2.20	Maths	Walberg (1984)
18	51.7	30.7	3.6	5.83	Maths	Husen (1967)

been more usually employed in its alternative mode of operation of cumulative deficit. This is the process by which environmentally disadvantaged groups tend to suffer cognitive deterioration over the years of childhood and adolescence. The phenomenon has been most fully worked out by Jensen (1977). In the case of the educational standards of Japanese children it appears that cumulative advantage is operating and reflects the beneficial impact of an advantageous environment operating cumulatively over the years of childhood and adolescence.

2.7 CONCLUSIONS

In this chapter the mean scores on tests of mathematics and science obtained by eight samples of Japanese school children have been reviewed and compared with those from various countries from the economically advanced West. In all eight samples the Japanese children have achieved higher scores than their Western counterparts. The Japanese lead increases over the years of childhood until by mid-adolescence Japanese teenagers are at least one standard deviation ahead of their contemporaries in the West. This lead represents approximately three years of schooling, so that the average Japanese 12-year-old is approximately at the same academic level as the average 15-year-old in the West. The steady increase of educational standards in Japan relative to those in the West indicates superior input of various factors, and it is to the nature of these factors that we now turn.

3 The Japanese School System

3.1 KINDERGARTEN

Compulsory education in Japan starts when children are aged six, as in most other countries. Britain is unusual in requiring compulsory education from the age of five. But the great majority of pre-school children in Japan attend voluntary kindergarten from the ages of three or four. The numbers attending kindergarten have risen steadily since the end of the Second World War. By 1980 approximately 85 per cent of pre-school children attended kindergarten nationally, and in Tokyo and other large cities the figure was over 90 per cent. In Britian and the USA about 40 per cent of 4-year-olds attend kindergarten.

There are both private and state kindergarten in Japan. Approximately 75 per cent are private and the remaining 25 per cent are state. Private kindergarten receive approximately 66 per cent of their revenue from fees, about 5 per cent from state subsidies, and the remainder from private sources such as endowments, loans and so forth. State kindergarten charge modest fees which contribute approximately 8 per cent of their revenue and the remainder of their costs are met by the local authority in which the school is situated.

Japanese kindergarten are not simply play schools, but provide an academic curriculum which includes the first stages of reading and arithmetic. Japanese children are expected to be able to read and do simple sums involving addition and subtraction by the time they leave kindergarten. Many Japanese mothers also devote time to teaching their young children of kindergarten age the basics of reading and arithmetic (Tanner, 1977). This early grounding at kindergarten and at home is largely responsible for ensuring that by the age of six, in their first term of compulsory primary schools, Japanese children are already well ahead of American children in arithmetic (Stigler, Lee, Lucker and Stevenson, 1982; Lynn and Hampson, 1986a, b and c).

In addition to teaching the first stages of reading and arithmetic, many Japanese kindergarten also attempt to develop the more general intellectual skills of thinking, observation, learning and general intelligence. One of the principal means for doing this is by the use of the *IQ Box*. This is a kit for training and practice in thinking and problem solving which is widely sold and used in Japan, both in kindergarten and in homes, and has no counterpart in Western countries. The widespread use of this kit is probably one reason for the acceleration of the intelligence of young Japanese children, relative to their Western counterparts, which will be discussed in Chapter 4.

While Japanese kindergarten as a whole typically place more emphasis on the intellectual and educational development of young children than do their counterparts in Britain, the United States and other Western countries, there are in addition a small number of academic hot-house private kindergarten in Tokyo and other cities which aim to provide an especially accelerated intellectual development. These cater for a limited market of parents who hope to secure their children's admission, at the age of six, to one of the academically strong private schools. A child who obtains entry into one of these stands a good chance of getting into an academically élite secondary high school, and from thence in turn to an élite university. Thus attendance at an academic private kindergarten is the first link in a chain which, if all goes well, will ultimately secure academic success at university level.

This element of private élite schooling in Japan is quite similar to the corresponding system in Britain, where there are also academically selective private kindergarten in London and other major cities which prepare children for academic private preparatory schools, which in turn facilitate entry to the academic independent schools, which in their turn confer an advantage in obtaining admission to the élite universities of Oxford and Cambridge. In both Japan and Britain the leading private academic kindergarten have considerable reputations among professional parents in their localities. They have more applicants than places and can afford to be selective in their intake. They maintain their standards and reputations for academic results partly by stringent selection procedures involving intelligence and other tests, and some Japanese private academic kindergarten administer intelligence tests to their applicants' mothers as well as to the children themselves. This is quite a sensible procedure from the point of view of schools wishing to sustain their reputations for academic excellence, since the intelligence of mothers is quite highly associated with that of their children and children's intelligence is obviously an important determinant of their subsequent educational achievement.

One of the chief points of general interest at this early stage of Japanese education concerns the very large numbers of Japanese parents who are willing to pay the fees to send their young children to kindergarten. Approximately 70 per cent of Japanese parents voluntarily pay these quite appreciable fees, so that it is not only the middle class but also a substantial section of the working class who are willing to meet these expenses. In Britain there is a strong demand for greater provision of kindergarten, but this takes the form of political lobbying for these to be provided by government. The demand is not apparently sufficiently strong for parents themselves to be willing to pay for these kindergarten, otherwise they would be established spontaneously by educational entrepreneurs. The same is true of the demand for more kindergarten in the United States. Yet Japanese parents do not have greater disposable incomes than British or American parents. Their greater willingness to devote their income to the payment of kindergarten fees is an early indication of a greater motivation and commitment by Japanese parents to their children's education that is generally present in the West.

3.2 PRIMARY SCHOOLS

Between the ages of 6 and 11 years almost all Japanese children attend their neighbourhood co-educational state primary schools for a six year period. Nationally 99.5 per cent of children attend these state primary schools and only 0.5 per cent attend private schools (these are 1980 figures, given by Mombusho, 1980). In the large cities the proportions of children attending private schools are somewhat greater, while in the rural areas where state schools enjoy a natural monopoly they are attended by virtually all children.

Japanese state primary schools are socially fairly heterogeneous. There is naturally some tendency in the cities for some districts to be largely middle class and others largely working class and here the social mix of the schools reflects that of their catchment area, but residential segregation by social class in not particularly pronounced in Japan. The situation is broadly similar to that in Britain. The social classes are much more segregated in the United States, where there are ethnic minority and impoverished white schools in many of the inner cities and virtually all white middle-class schools in satellite dormitory towns.

The small number of Japanese private primary schools are nearly all so-called university schools. These are schools attached to a particular university. Children can enter them at the age of six and normally, conditional on satisfactory academic progress, remain there throughout their school education until they reach the age of eighteen. In addition these schools generally admit a further intake at the age of 12 to their secondary school section. These university schools are academically strong and among the most prestigious schools in Japan and there is considerable competition to get into them. Besides providing a strong academic education these university schools operate preferential admission policies to their own universities, so that a child who gains admission to one of these schools at the age of six stands a good chance in due course of getting into the university under whose aegis the school is run.

3.3 THE CURRICULUM

The curriculum taught in Japanese schools is laid down by central government through the Ministry of Education. The Ministry stipulates the academic syllabus that has to be covered by each age group during the school year, and also the number of hours in the year that each subject has to be taught. The syllabus is set out in considerable detail in a series of lengthy handbooks of some two hundred pages for each academic subject for each grade. The Ministry also issues lists of recommended text books from which schools can choose the ones they wish to adopt. In Britain and the United States schools have much more autonomy and the syllabus is largely determined by head teachers.

The detail of the curriculum laid down by the Japanese government has both similarities and differences from that typically followed in the West. Much of the curriculum consists of the familiar school subjects of language and literature, mathematics, science, foreign languages, history, geography and social studies. In addition, there are two further subjects which are taught more thoroughly in Japan than in the West. The first is music, which is compulsory from the start of schooling, 6-year-olds learn to play the recorder, 7-year-olds typically learn a wind instrument and 10-year-olds frequently learn to play a third instrument. All Japanese children are taught to read music and by the ages of ten and eleven they are formed into orchestras. Music continues to be a compulsory subject in Japanese secondary schools right up to the age of eighteen.

The second subject which is taught much more thoroughly in Japanese schools than in the West is moral education. This also is a compulsory subject for Japanese children from the age of six and throughout their schooling. The objective here is to make children morally aware and to foster their moral development. The lessons in moral education are both theoretical and practical. One of the commonest forms of teaching is for children to watch a film. The teacher then discusses the moral problems raised by the film with the class. Practical moral education takes the form of requiring children to do the domestic work of the school, such as serving, clearing up school lunches and the school cleaning. Japanese schools do not have the paid cleaners who do the cleaning in British and American schools. The children themselves and the teachers do the cleaning. Although this clearly has the advantage of saving money, the primary purpose is moral. It conveys to children such lessons as that if they throw down sweet papers and other rubbish, it is they themselves who have to go round and pick it up later. It is intended to foster a collective sense of moral responsibility for the cleanliness and appearance of the school and that everyone should make a contribution to this end. It is an interesting question whether schools in the West might not usefully adopt these Japanese practices.

3.4 JUNIOR HIGH SCHOOLS

At the age of eleven to twelve Japanese children leave their primary schools and proceed to secondary schools, as do almost all children at or about this age in the West. However, the Japanese system is unusual in splitting secondary schooling into two stages consisting of junior high schools and senior high schools. Each stage lasts three years, namely from the ages of approximately 12 to 14 and 15 to 18. Most of these secondary schools are co-educational, but there are also significant numbers of single sex schools.

The majority of Japanese children pass automatically from their neighbourhood primary school to their neighbourhood junior high school. A small minority of parents do switch their children at this stage from public to private schools. The reason for this is that they perceive the private schools are providing a better academic education. But the numbers making this switch into private education amount to only approximately 3 per cent of Japanese children in this age range. This figure is lower than the 6 per cent of British children and 13 per cent of American children in private schools.

Japanese 12- to 14-year-olds at the junior high schools work exceedingly hard. They are entering the period of their lives known awesomely as *examination hell* and Japanese folklore has it that those who sleep more than four hours a night cannot hope to succeed in the intense competition for academic success that lies ahead. The first important hurdle has to be faced in only some two and a half years' time when, at the age of fourteen, they take the entrance examinations to senior high schools.

It is at this point that the Japanese school system assumes a new aspect which differentiates it sharply from the earlier stages and from school systems in the West. Japanese senior high schools, which cater for the 15–18 year age range, are hierarchically ranked for their academic quality by the public in each locality. It is considered vital for a successful career to secure entry to a good senior high school as the first step on the ladder to an élite university and from there into a high status job in the civil service, the professions or in one of the large corporations. This makes doing well in the 'fourteen plus' entrance examinations for senior high schools crucially important for Japanese teenagers, and is the principal factor responsible for the hard work they put into their academic studies at junior high school.

At the completion of their junior high schools at the age of fourteen to fifteen, Japanese teenagers have three options open to them. Firstly, they are permitted at this age to cease education altogether and enter employment. However, the proportion proceeding voluntarily to some form of further education has risen gradually in the post-World War Two decades from approximately 50 per cent in the 1950s to 94 per cent by 1980. The low figure of 6 per cent who opt to end their education can be compared with the 52 per cent (in 1983) who leave school in Britain at the age if sixteen, as soon as the law permits. This difference is the more striking because in Japan all education from the age of sixteen onwards requires fees, whereas in Britain it is free. The much higher proportion of adolescents in Japan who are willing to continue their education voluntarily, and of parents who are willing to pay their fees, is a testimony to the widespread commitment to education in Japan.

The second option for Japanese 15-year-olds is to embark on a course of vocational education in a vocational school or college. The third option is to continue their academic education in a senior high school.

3.5 SUPPLEMENTARY EDUCATION: THE JUKU

Since the 'fourteen plus' examinations for entry to selective senior high schools are so important in Japan, it may be thought surprising that there is not a larger proportion of private junior high schools specialising in teaching for success in these examinations. It may be wondered why academic private junior high schools have not been founded to meet parental demand for a strong academic education. There are three principal reasons why this has not occurred. Firstly, Japanese public junior high schools themselves provide a strong academic education. Secondly, public junior high schools in middle-class districts are academically stronger than those in working-class districts, as of course they are in Britain and the United States. Middle-class parents with their greater financial resources have therefore tended to move into residential areas where there are strong academic schools. In this way they are able to secure a strong academic education for their children at minimal cost. Information on the academic quality of schools is more extensive in Japan than in the West because the press reports and analyses the examination results of schools in considerable detail. Parents therefore have a good knowledge of where the strongest public schools are and tend to locate their homes accordingly.

The third reason that private academic junior high schools have not been founded is that an extensive system of private schools have been established to meet parental demand but instead of replacing public schools they operate alongside them. The way in which this unexpected development has evolved is as follows. Schools work relatively short hours and enjoy long holidays in Japan, as they do in the West. It is therefore quite feasible for parents ambitious for their children's academic success – and there are a lot of such parents in Japan – to have their children attend two schools, a public school during the normal working school day and term, and a private school during the evenings, weekends and school holidays. In this way large numbers of Japanese parents secure the maximum educational advantage for their children, not by withdrawing their children from the public schools but by supplementing public school education with additional education at private schools.

These supplementary private schools are known as *juku*. These *juku* cater for children of all ages. There are *juku* for children of primary school age who are attempting to gain entry to one of the private academic junior high schools. Greater numbers of children enrol at later ages and large numbers of 12- to 14-year-olds attend *juku* for additional coaching for the 'fourteen plus' entrance examinations to the senior high schools. There are also many 15- to 18-year-olds who attend *juku* for coaching for the university entrance examinations.

These *juku* have evolved gradually over the course of decades. Initially, in the 1920s and 1930s, the *juku* were quite modest establishments and consisted typically of retired or moonlighting schoolteachers taking a few pupils for additional coaching in their own homes during the evenings and in school holidays. These early *juku* resembled similar small enterprises in Britain where coaching for the 'eleven plus' examination used to be given to individual or small groups of children. These cottage industry *juku* still exist in Japan, but alongside them there have also grown up large scale enterprises with purpose-built four or five storey buildings and operated by national chains. These are highly professional businesses whose objective is to beat the examination system for high school and university entrance. Among them there are now élite *juku* which specialise in the entrance examinations for the élite high schools and the élite universities. These have their own entrance examinations and admit only able and promising pupils who are likely to do well and be a credit to the school. In some cases attendance at an élite *juku* carries almost as much status as attendance at an élite high school or university.

The great growth of these highly professional *juku* has been largely a post-war phenomenon, and they now play an important role in Japanese education. The Japanese Ministry of Education carried out a survey of *juku* in 1976. This showed that over half of 12–14-year-olds were enrolled in *juku* in Tokyo, Osaka and other large cities. The proportions of 9- to 11-year-olds attending *juku* is somewhat less, namely about 20 per cent. More boys are enrolled than girls, reflecting the greater importance attached by Japanese parents to the education of boys, but the percentages are not greatly disparate between the sexes.

Japanese adolescents spend an appreciable proportion of time at their *juku*. Typically they attend two or three evenings a week and on Saturday afternoons. In the school holidays attendance at the *juku* becomes full-time. Thus for large numbers of Japanese children the *juku* have assumed an importance almost as great as that of their ordinary schools.

The *juku* do not receive any form of government subsidy. They are purely commerical enterprises engaged in selling education to consumers like any other service sold by commercial businesses. The *juku* constitute an interesting and, to many Western observers, unexpected adaptation of the market to the needs of Japanese parents, who are able to secure a free education at the public schools topped up by additional education purchased at *juku*. In their essentially supplementary role to publically funded or subsidised ordinary schools they bear some conceptual resemblance to pensions in the West, where a basic public service is provided for everyone, but which increasing numbers of citizens choose to supplement with additional private schemes which they purchase in the market.

3.6 SENIOR HIGH SCHOOLS

From the age of fifteen about two-thirds of Japanese teenagers who continue their education voluntarily do so in an academic senior high school and the remaining third in a vocational high school or college. The academic senior high schools are the preferred choice of the great majority. These schools have higher social status than the vocational schools and they lead to entry to university, to which very large numbers of Japanese teenagers and their parents aspire.

The curriculum in the senior high schools continues to be laid down by the Ministry of Education. It is broader than that for the corresponding age group in Britain. All pupils have to study Japanese literature and history, English, social studies, science and mathematics, but some specialisation is also allowed in subjects to be taken for the university entrance examinations.

The Japanese senior high schools have a number of interesting features. The first is that, as noted above, in every locality the school's standing is determined by the examination results of its pupils. These results are not obtained from successes in public examinations like the British General Certificate of Education (GCE), for which there is no equivalent in Japan. They are derived from the school's successes in the entry examinations to the University of Tokyo or a small handful of other prestigious universities.

A Japanese professor of education has described this system as follows:

There is a hierarchy of high schools. The number of students that high schools are able to place in universities with good reputations determines the high school's repute. Hence, high ranking schools are selective and admit only those students with good scholastic records and excellent examination skills. The quality of teaching staff and the school environment have relatively little influence on ranking. Every prefecture and major city has a hierarchy of high schools determined solely by this criterion. (Shimahara, 1979)

Normally in Japan the schools have their own entrance examinations and control their own admissions, although in some cities the public authorities set the entrance examinations and allocate children to the public high schools on the basis of the candidates' results. In addition to examination performance, schools take into account reports from the principals of the pupils' junior high schools, but as these reports are largely based on the pupils' performance in a series of mock entrance examinations they for the most part simply confirm the results of the examinations themselves.

To some degree the hierarchical ranking of Japanese senior high schools in public esteem has parallels in Britain, the United States and Continental Europe. For instance, in London the three most prestigious schools would generally be considered to be Westminster, St Paul's and Dulwich; below these stand a number of other independent schools such as Emanuel, the City of London School, etc.; and below these stand the state comprehensive schools, some of which will be judged by the population to be better than others. There are similar hierarchies in the major cities throughout most of Continental Europe. In the United States the hierarchical ranking of schools is much less pronounced, although even in the USA the population make distinctions between the local high schools.

But while in all countries some schools are more highly regarded than others, the hierarchical ranking of senior high schools in Japan is far more powerfully present in the public mind than it is elsewhere. Two significant features of the ranking of the senior high schools in Japan are the precise quantifications of the schools' academic excellence and the publicity which is accorded to schools' academic results. The criteria for assessing schools' academic merit is the success of their pupils in obtaining entry to the University of Tokyo and a dozen or so other élite universities. The University of Tokyo is the most prestigious in Japan, where it occupies a position broadly comparable to the universities of Oxford and Cambridge in Britain, Harvard and Yale in the United States and the Ecole Polytechnique in France. The university admits approximately 3000 students a year, of which about 93 per cent are male. It is the ambition of nearly all able Japanese boys and of their parents to secure a place at Tokyo or, failing this, at one of another dozen or so highly prestigious universities.

Each year a complete list of the names of those obtaining entry to the University of Tokyo and to the other élite universities are published in the Japanese press. On the basis of these results senior high schools are ranked in order of their success in obtaining places at the University of Tokyo, and elsewhere. A number of the top schools in Japan succeed in placing around half, or even more, of their graduating classes at the University of Tokyo, and most of the remainder in other prestige universities. The Japanese press publishes performance league tables of the élite schools' successes going back twenty years and plots the rising achievements of some schools and the decline of others. Even schools placing one pupil at Tokyo University are listed in the Japanese newspapers.

It is difficult to convey to the Western reader the enormous public interest taken in the annual rankings of these élite Japanese senior high schools. The public follow avidly the achievements of the leading schools, somewhat as they do of sports teams in the West, such as those of cricket and football teams in England whose results are announced in regular radio and television news bulletins. So in Japan the performance of the leading senior high schools is closely monitored and extensively reported by the media. Thus for a string of years in the 1950s and 1960s the top position was regularly taken by Hibiya High School in Tokyo, which succeeded in placing virtually the whole of its graduating classes in Tokyo University, or in a handful of other élite universities. At this time Hibiya came to be regarded as the best school in Japan. But from the early 1970s the school's successes began to fade. Initially Hibiya dropped to third or fourth place. Then it ceased to appear among the top ten and finally it did not even obtain a place among the top twenty. At the same time hitherto unknown schools began to appear in the annual rankings.

These reversals and successes in the fortunes of the leading senior high schools are the subject of great interest and discussion in the media. The head masters are interviewed on television and in the press and the reasons for the school's success or failure are probed and analysed. It is as if the middlebrow press in Britain were to print as a lead story that this year Eton had overtaken Manchester Grammar School in the number of boys gaining places at Oxford and Cambridge, or in the United States that more boys had secured entry to Harvard and Yale from Groton than from Exeter – , schools which few Americans have ever heard of.

The intense and much publicised competition between senior high schools has important psychological effects on both pupils and teachers. Three of these in particular can be noted. Firstly, it promotes considerable public prestige for the University of Tokyo and a dozen or so other élite universities and generates widespread motivation among large numbers of teenagers to secure admission to one of these prestigious institutions. This is one of the sources of the high motivation for academic work that characterises Japanese teenagers. Secondly, the hierarchical ranking applies to all the schools in each locality. We note here an important difference between Japan and Britain. In Britain there are one or two academically élite schools in every city, for example, the Royal Grammar School in Newcastle-upon-Tyne, King Edward VI's School in Birmingham and so forth. But apart from these private schools which are of interest to only around 10 per cent of the population, the remaining state comprehensive schools are all much of a muchness. In London the pupil intakes are controlled by the local authority specifically to prevent a status hierarchy of academic excellence from emerging. This is secured by allocating children to schools in such a way that the average intelligence level of the pupils at each school is approximately the same.

In Japan it is not a mere handful of schools that are hierarchically ranked for academic excellence, but all schools. The effect of this is that all Japanese 14-year-olds are provided with the incentive to attempt to obtain entry to as good a school as possible. The most able will naturally aim to get into the best school in the locality. Those of modest ability aim to get into a middle-ranking school. Entry to all schools is by competitive examination. Hence it is quite possible for a Japanese teenager to fail to get into any senior high school at all and this does in fact happen. For large numbers of Japanese teenagers obtaining entry to a senior high school is therefore a privilege that has to be worked for during the years at junior high schools. There is a contrast here with British and American 15- and 16-year-olds, many of whom are unwilling conscripts in the school system into which they are coerced by the criminal law.

A third effect of the hierarchical ranking of senior high schools in Japan is that it generates competition not only between school children to secure admission to high status schools, but also between the schools to secure able pupils. The psychological impact of the system is felt here by the teachers. The publicity given to schools' educational achievements presents a challenge to teachers to produce good academic results. Teachers' self-esteem and pride become bound up with the educational achievements of their schools and this acts as a motivator to teach efficiently and to maintain or improve the academic standards. Teachers are not placed on their mettle in this way in the West, where there is no precise public knowledge of the academic excellence or otherwise of schools. The high public visibility of schools' academic achievements in Japan acts as a considerable incentive to teachers to produce good results, and this is undoubtedly an important reason for the high levels of professionalism and commitment among Japanese teachers which are documented later in this book. At this stage we note only that the Japanese 'fourteen plus' examinations for entry to hierarchically ranked senior high schools have important motivating effects for both pupils and teachers, which are largely absent in other countries.

3.7 PUBLIC AND PRIVATE SENIOR HIGH SCHOOLS

An unusual feature of the senior high school in Japan is that a large proportion of them are private institutions. Over Japan as a whole, approximately 30 per cent of the senior high schools are private, but in the major cities the proportion is higher. In Tokyo approximately 60 per cent of the senior high schools are private. In Osaka-Kobe, the second largest conurbation in Japan, some 50 per cent of senior high schools are private, and 45 per cent are private in the city of Kyoto. On the other hand, in rural areas the proportion of private senior high schools drops to between 5 and 10 per cent. The overall proportion of 30 per cent of senior high schools in the private sector in Japan can be compared with the figures noted previously of 6 per cent for private schools in Britian and 13 per cent in the United States. As private institutions, Japanese private senior high schools charge fees. Fees are also charged by the public senior high schools, but these are very low. Details of the financial aspects of the schools are given later.

It is impossible to make any simple generalisations about whether the public or the private senior high schools are better in academic quality. In this respect the situation in Japan does not resemble that in Britain, where by common consent the best schools are private and are either the old city day schools – Manchester Grammar School, St Paul's School in London and so forth – or the independent boarding schools such as Eton and Winchester. Statistical data showing the academic superiority of these British private schools as compared with the state schools has been presented for England by Marks and Pomain-Stzednicki (1985) and for Scotland by McPherson and Willms (1986).

The position in Japan is more complex. Both public and private senior high schools can be found at all levels of the hierarchical rank order which is present in all Japanese cities and towns. Both types of school are represented among the top twenty most prestigious schools in Japan, and also among middle-ranking and poorly regarded schools. In recent years, however, the private high schools have considerably improved their position among the best high schools in Japan at the expense of the public high schools. The reasons for this are set out in the next section.

Historically, in the earlier decades of the century, the public high schools were the more highly regarded. Indeed, in the pre-1945 period and for some years after the war the best schools in Japan were by universal consent the leading public high schools. Each major city in Japan had at least one strong academic public high school, and in many cases several. They charged only nominal fees and selected their entrants by their own entrance examinations from the ablest boys and girls in the locality. These schools occupied a position quite similar to that of the former British direct grant schools, which were also generally the academically strongest and prestigious schools in their localities and were able, through their free places and subsidised fees, to admit the most able children in their respective localities irrespective of the parents' means and social position.

The leading example of an academically élite public senior high school was Hibiya School in Tokyo, to which reference was made above. Hibiya admitted a large proportion of the cleverest boys from the whole of Tokyo and the surrounding suburbs. Throughout the 1950s and 1960s, Hibiya generally came first in the annual ranking of Japanese senior high schools for places obtained at the University of Tokyo.

The high standing of Hibiya and other élite senior public high schools was largely self-sustaining. They were able to be highly selective in their admissions and take only the most intelligent and academically motivated boys and girls. The whole intake could be given an academically rigorous course and by the age of eighteen they had reached the academic standard achieved by typical American university graduates at the age of twenty-two. Virtually the whole of the graduating classes did well in the university entrance examinations. Admitting pupils at the age of 14/15 ensured that the selection procedures were less subject to error than in Britain, where boys and girls are normally admitted to the independent day secondary schools at the age of eleven, and to the independent boarding schools at the age of thirteen. There is no exact counterpart in Britain to the position held by Hibiya and similar élite academic high schools in Japan. In some respects the closest parallel is Manchester Grammar School, often regarded as the best academic school in Britain because its boys regularly win the greatest number of open scholarships to Oxford and Cambridge. On the other hand, many people would consider that the best schools in Britain are Eton and Winchester, which are élite schools socially as well as academically. Japan does not possess socially élite schools of this kind. The sole criterion for the public standing of the schools is their academic excellence.

In the pre-war and early post-war years, public high schools like Hibiya existed in all Japanese cities and towns. Since these schools were academically excellent and also cheap, Japanese parents were only too happy to send their children to them. There was, however, a problem. This was that many more parents wanted their children to go to these schools than there were places available. Inevitably there were many parents who were disappointed when their children failed the entrance examinations to one of these schools. In these cases the children were obliged to go instead to a more poorly regarded school and this was something that many parents did not like.

This problem was similar to that prevailing in Britain during the period of approximately 1944–1975, when children took the 'eleven plus' examination for entry to direct grant schools, maintained grammar schools and secondary modern schools. In Britain also there were children who failed the examination and therefore had to go to the poorly regarded secondary modern schools. In both Britain and Japan parents were unhappy when their children failed these entrance examinations to prestigious academic schools, and in both countries this situation led to the same result. This was the foundation or strengthening of a number of private fee paying secondary schools catering for middle-class parents of children who failed the examinations to the public academic secondary schools. In both countries these private schools aimed to provide a reasonably sound second best academic education for the children of middle-class parents who were able to afford the fees. These private fee paying high schools might hopefully give a sufficiently good education to enable their pupils to gain admission to one of the better universities, and at the same time they provided a shelter from the hurly-burly of the less good public high schools with their large working-class intakes. These private high schools in Japan therefore served a similar purpose to that of a number of private secondary schools in Britain, to which some middle-class parents used to send their children if they failed the 'eleven plus' examination to a state grammar school. In both Japan and Britain they catered for pupils of only average ability and obtained indifferent academic results.

Thus, in the inter-war period, and for a time following World War Two, the private schools in Japan occupied an inferior position in academic reputation and public esteem. The schools with the highest standing were the élite public high schools, many of them with solid academic reputations going back into the last century. So high was the repute of the leading public high schools that it would have seemed a wellnigh impossible task to dethrone them from their position at the apex of Japan's secondary school system. Yet this is precisely what has occurred over the last quarter century.

3.8 THE RISE OF THE PRIVATE SENIOR HIGH SCHOOLS

The rise of the private senior high schools in the post-war decades and particularly after the mid-1960s has come about through the comprehensivisation of the public senior high schools. In Japan, as in Britain and much of Continental Europe, both the Socialist Party and the teachers' union disliked the differentiation between élite academic schools, inevitably drawn largely from middle-class families, and poorly regarded low-ranking schools, mainly catering for working-class children. Their ideal was the neighbourhood comprehensive high school, based on the American model, which all children living in the school's residential catchment area would attend as of right. In this they were supported by a team of OECD international educational experts who carried out a survey of Japanese schools in 1971 and, in accordance with the egalitarian *Zeitgeist* of the time, recommended in their report that it would be desirable 'to minimise social differentiation' between schools and to promote 'more homogenous comprehensive schools rather than differentiate by ability between schools' (OECD, 1971).

In the pursuit of these ideals, when the Socialist Party gained power in the major Japanese cities it began to put its comprehensivisation programme into effect. It was quite simple to do this. All that was involved was to curtail the power of the élite academic high schools to select their pupil intakes from the whole of the city and to limit the intakes to the districts in which the schools were situated. This sufficed to turn the élite high schools into neighbourhood comprehensives. The effect of these new reforms was predictable. The academic results achieved by schools were to a considerable extent determined by the intelligence and home background of their pupils, although the commitment and professionalism of teachers also played its part. Once the élite public senior high schools had their power to select the ablest boys and girls from the whole of the cities in which they were situated removed and were transformed into neighbourhood comprehensives, the quality of their intakes fell. It was an inevitable consequence that the academic results of these schools, evaluated by the success of their pupils in gaining entry to the prestigious universities, were also bound to decline. At the same time, the quality of the intakes in the poorly regarded public schools tended to improve. Thus one of the effects of these comprehensivisation programmes was that the hierarchical structure of the public senior high schools was largely dismantled and replaced by an egalitarian structure. This was the objective of the programmes and to a considerable extent it was accomplished.

There was, however, a second effect which had not been so clearly foreseen. This was that as the academic quality of the élite public senior high schools declined, large numbers of predominantly middle-class parents responded by switching their children into the private high schools. This enabled the private schools to be more selective in their admission. The academic quality of their intakes improved and so too did their academic standards, and at the same time this depressed further the academic quality of the intakes into the public high schools. In Japan, where the academic standing of schools is so closely monitored by the media, these changes rapidly became public knowledge and the middle-class flight from the public high schools became a stampede.

The timing and administrative details of these comprehensivisation programmes varied from one Japanese city to another, according to when the Socialist Party gained power and chose to put the reorganisation into effect. One of the first cities to introduce comprehensivisation was the major provincial city of Nagoya. The leading academic public high school was called Umigaoka. It admitted many of the cleverest boys from a catchment area of several million people, achieved excellent academic results and was regularly placed among the top twenty schools of Japan each year. The comprehensivisation programme restricted the intake to Umigaoka to boys living in two areas of the city. As a consequence the academic results of the school plummeted and two private high schools took its place as the leading academic schools of the city.

Some of the most dramatic of these changes took place in Tokyo, where comprehensivisation was introduced in 1967. Historically there were three élite public senior high schools in Tokyo – Hibiya, Nishi and Koishikawa – and all three schools were placed regularly among the top twenty schools in Japan. As we have seen, Hibiya was generally at the top of the list and was regarded as the best high school in all Japan. All three schools took their pupils from all over Tokyo and the surrounding suburbs and were able to select boys of very high ability. The 1967 comprehensivisation programmes restricted the intake of these schools to the neighbourhoods in which they were located. The academic quality of their intakes fell drastically and so too did the academic results achieved by the schools. By 1976 two of the three élite schools, Hibiya and Koishikawa, had disappeared from the list of the nation's top twenty schools. Only Nishi, by virtue of the favourable catchment area in which it was located, just retained a position towards the bottom of the list. A variety of ingenious stratagems were adopted by a number of parents anxious to get their sons into Nishi. Some bought houses in the school's catchment area, while others took accommodation addresses, arranged for their sons to lodge nominally with relations or friends, or simply faked residence near the school to fulfil the new residential requirements. But most middle-class parents, who could afford the fees, began to send their children to the private high schools.

At the same time comprehensivisation programmes were being put into effect in a number of other Japanese cities. Generally these changes did not involve full comprehensivisation. The typical form of the new organisation was to divide the city into several districts. Each district was sufficiently large to contain a number of public senior high schools. Pupils were only permitted to attend a high school in the district in which they resided, but as there were a number of high schools in each district a hierarchy of academic standing estabished itself. The effect of this attenuated form of comprehensivisation has been that there are still a number of strong academic senior high schools in most Japanese cities. However, the restriction of the catchment area has resulted in some drop in the quality of the intakes of the very best schools and this has been sufficient to impair the academic results and reputations of a large number of them. This, in turn, has induced large numbers of middle-class Japanese parents to switch their children into the private senior high schools. The annual statistics of admissions to the University of Tokyo reveal the extent of the transformation of the relative positions of the public and private schools in the post-World War Two decades. In the 1950s the top twenty schools in the country were nearly all public high schools. By the mid-1980s about half of these had disappeared and the top twenty schools were approximately equally divided between public and private schools.

3.9 JAPAN'S LEADING SENIOR HIGH SCHOOL: NADA

As many of the public high schools fell in the 1970s from their pre-eminent status as Japan's leading academic schools and their position was taken by private schools, the front runner to emerge as the top academic school in Japan was a hitherto obscure school called Nada. An excellent description of this school has been given by the American anthropologist T. P. Rohlen (1983). It is a school that few had ever heard of before 1960, even in Japan, and it is situated not in Tokyo but in a suburb of the provincial city of Kobe. The school takes only boys and admits some boarders, but most of its pupils are day boys living in Kobe and neighbouring Osaka, which are about 250 hundred miles west of Tokyo and together form the second largest conurbation in Japan. The position of Nada in Japan is not altogether unlike that of Manchester Grammar school in Britain, where what is perhaps the foremost British academic school is situated not in London but one of the country's major provincial cities.

Nada was founded in 1928 by endowments provided by three local *sake* brewers. At this period there were several strong academic public senior high schools of high repute in Kobe and these were the first choice for able teenagers of all social classes, as was the case generally throughout Japan at this period. Only those who failed the entrance examinations for these public high schools were sent to Nada by middle-class families able to afford the fees. The school was academically undistinguished and the pupils were normally only able to gain admission to second and third rank universities.

The change in Nada's fortunes came about in the 1950s, when the Kobe local authority introduced a comprehensivisation policy for the public high schools. Kobe was one of the first cities in Japan to turn its élite public senior high schools into comprehensives. Parents of gifted children were no longer able to send them to the élite public high schools unless they happened to live in the appropriate residential district. A number of these therefore turned to Nada. This enabled the school to become more selective in its intake and the school's academic standing began to rise as increasing numbers of its pupils started to gain admission to Tokyo University and other high status universities.

From the mid-1960s Nada began to appear in the annual lists of the top twenty schools in Japan. As comprehensivisation policies progressively undermined the academic achievements of the public high schools, so the standing of Nada increased further. From the mid-1970s Nada has generally been placed either top or second among the nation's senior high schools. In a typical year about half its final year students obtain entry to the University of Tokyo, and almost all the rest secure admission to other universities of high standing.

There are two intakes at Nada. Three-quarters of its pupils enter the school at the ages of 11/12 years for a six year course. Hence Nada combines in one school the age range usually divided into junior and senior high schools in Japan. The school takes approximately 165 boys a year at the ages of 11/12. A further 55 are admitted at the ages of 14/15 years for the final three year course leading to university entrance.

As the academic reputation of the school has grown the demand for places has increased and entry is now very competitive. It is estimated that to have even a chance of admission a boy has to be comfortably in the top 1 per cent of the ability range and that of these only one in three is actually admitted to the school. Academic standards at the school are very high and the boys have a strong sense of being part of an élite. Given the public interest in élite schools in Japan, journalists quite frequently interview boys from the school and ask them what they intend to be when they are grown up. There is always one who gives the inevitable reply – 'Prime Minister'.

The school is strictly meritocratic and does not have the element of social class exclusiveness which characterises the leading British and American private boarding schools. Entry is secured solely on performance in the entrance examinations, supplemented by the reports of the primary school head teachers. Fees are relatively modest, so that a large number of parents can afford to send their boys to the school. However, children's academic achievement in Japan, as in the West generally, is quite strongly associated with socioeconomic status, and Nada boys come mainly from professional and managerial families. The school does not achieve its outstanding academic results through superior resources. Class sizes number approximately 55, which would of course be considered very large in Britain, the United States and throughout Continental Europe. This size of class is typical in Japan, but teachers spend fewer hours teaching, and staff/pupil ratios in Japan are not much greater than those generally prevailing in the West.

The meteoric rise of Nada from provincial obscurity to national pre-eminence over the last twenty years or so has generated great public interest in Japan. There are frequent newspaper and magazine articles on the school, containing discussions of the reasons for its success and interviews with boys and their parents. A novel has been written about the school and serialised in a weekly magazine.

It is difficult to convey to Western readers the drama that has accompanied the rise of the private high schools, among which Nada is the foremost example, and the corresponding downfall of the famous academic public high schools over the last twenty years or so. What has occurred in Japan in somewhat as if in Britian the most famous élite schools, such as Eton, Harrow, Winchester and Rugby and so on, which have figured so prominently in the nation's history and literature, were to be turned into neighbourhood comprehensives, their academic, historical and social reputations destroyed, to be replaced over the course of a few years by a new group of élite schools which previously few people had ever heard of.

3.10 CONTEMPORARY STANDING OF PUBLIC AND PRIVATE SENIOR HIGH SCHOOLS

By the 1980s the comprehensivisation of the public senior high schools in Japan had been largely completed. This programme disturbed the rank order of the senior high schools in terms of academic excellence and the new rank order to emerge can be described in the following broad terms. The foremost academic high schools in most Japanese cities are now one or two private schools. Below these are some strong academic public high schools. These are the top schools in the mini-hierarchies of some half a dozen public schools in the districts into which cities are normally divided. There are also typically some private senior high schools at this level. Further down the hierarchies and right down to the bottom there are both public and private high schools. The number of places in the public senior high schools is limited so that not every 15-year-old can secure entry. There are many parents in Japan who wish their children to continue their education at senior high school and would prefer them to do this at a poorly regarded public school than at a poorly regarded private high school. The reason for this is that the fees are substantially less. Hence there is competition to gain admission even into low ranking schools. Nevertheless, there are many Japanese parents who are willing to pay the fees for their children to continue their education even in low ranking private high schools, in the hope of furthering their career prospects.

The comprehensivisation programmes which were carried through in most Japanese cities from the 1960s onwards had the paradoxical effect of increasing the educational advantages of middle-class children and decreasing those of working-class children. The reason for this is that exceptionally intelligent children from poor families were formerly able to secure entry to the academically élite public senior high schools and their parents were able to pay the nominal fees. The comprehensivisation programmes resulted in private schools becoming the academically élite schools, and poorer parents were unable to pay the fees. Broadly, only middle-class parents could afford the fees for the élite private high schools and in this way they gained an advantage. This result can be described as paradoxical because the objective of the comprehensive reorganisation was to reduce social inequalities, but its effect has been to promote them.

The advantage which comprehensivisation entailed for middle-class children is reflected in the changing proportions of the student intake at the University of Tokyo coming from public and private schools. In 1960 private school pupils obtained 10 per cent of places at the university, considerably less than their due proportion, since approximately 30 per cent of pupils attended private senior high schools. By 1975, private senior high schools had obtained *per capita* parity with state schools, obtaining approximately 30 per cent of places. By 1982 the private senior high schools had pulled ahead, obtaining 48 per cent of places.

There are close parallels in the effects of comprehensivisation on reducing equality of opportunity between Japan and Britain. In Britain, as in Japan, the state grammar schools and direct grant schools were free to intellectually able children from working-class families in the period from 1944 to the 1970s. The abolition of this free access to élite academic schools in the mid-1970s has cut off this route to upward social mobility for working-class children, and likewise resulted in a system which is more differentiated by social class and is less meritocratic.

3.11 STATE SUBSIDIES TO PRIVATE SCHOOLS

It has been noted that approximately 30 per cent of the senior high schools in Japan are private fee paying institutions. This is a far greater percentage than that in Britain, the United States or in Continental

Europe generally, and it may be wondered how it is that such a large proportion of Japanese parents are able to afford the fees to send their children to these private schools. The answer is that the private schools receive subsidies from government. These subsidies are of two principal kinds. Capital grants are given for projects authorised by the Ministry of Education, for example new laboratory buildings for science and computers, audio-visual equipment and so forth. By far the largest item of state subsidy, however, is that given for the salaries of teachers. The government pays approximately 50 per cent of the salary costs of private schools. These payments are conditional on the school meeting minimum standards in buildings and tuition, which are assessed by inspectors. Teachers' salaries are the greatest item in school expenditure in Japan, as in other countries, so that the private schools are subsidised to the extent of approaching half of their costs. The remainder is met by fees which typically contribute around 60 per cent of total school expenditures.

These state subsidies to private schools in Japan are given in broadly the same way as they were in Britain to the direct grant schools before government financial assistance for these was withdrawn in the mid-1970s. The government subsidies ensure that the cost to parents of sending their children to private senior high schools is substantially less than in Britain and the United States, and is the reason why so many more Japanese parents are able to afford to send their children to private schools. It is difficult to convey the costs of fees for Japanese senior high schools in these times of inflation and fluctuating exchange rates (annual fees of around 350 000 yen will probably mean little to the average British or American reader). An approximate rule of thumb for estimating the fees at Japanese senior high schools is as follows. The cost of running a school in Japan is about the same as in Britain, and Japanese parents pay in fees about 60 per cent of this cost. It follows that school fees in Japan at any particular time run at about 60 per cent of those generally prevailing in Britain. At the time of writing (1986), fees at British private (independent) day secondary schools are on average approximately £2500 per annum, and fees at Japanese senior high schools are therefore around £1500 per annum. In addition to the fees being lower, Japanese parents opting for private senior high schools have a further advantage over British parents in that they only have to find these fees for three years, since the great majority of Japanese senior high schools are only three year schools (as has been noted, for adolescents aged 15/18) and these schools are generally entered from the free public junior high schools. In Britain parents opting for private secondary schools have to find fees for seven years (in the case of the independent day schools), since the children must enter the schools at the age of 11, and in addition it is normally necessary to go to private junior schools from the ages of 5 or 7 to 11 in order to cover the syllabus necessary to pass the entrance examination for entry to the independent secondary schools. In the case of the independent British boarding schools (ie 'public schools' such as Eton, Winchester and so forth) the parents are also committed to fee paying for a period of eleven years. It is evident, therefore, that the Japanese system imposes far less of a financial burden on parents and consequently many more parents in Japan are able to afford to send their children to private schools, at the senior secondary stage, although fewer do so earlier.

The public senior high schools in Japan also charge fees although these are considerably lower than in private schools. The Japanese Ministry of Education, Science and Culture gives a figure of 60 000 yen per annum as the average fee, approximately one-sixth of private senior high school fees, and representing approximately £250 in 1986 pounds sterling.

Loans are available to students attending both private and public senior high schools. These loans can be obtained from a variety of sources including the Japan Scholarship Foundation, local authorities and local charitable foundations. The largest source of loans is the Japan Scholarship Foundation. In 1980/81 it gave average loans to students at public senior high schools of 84 000 yen per annum (representing approximately £300 p.a.) and at private senior high schools of 216 000 yen per annum (approximately £720 p.a.). Thus these loans cover slightly more than the fees at public senior high schools but rather less than the fees at the private senior high schools.

3.12 VOCATIONAL HIGH SCHOOLS AND TECHNICAL COLLEGES

It was noted in an earlier section that Japanese 15-year-olds have three options. Firstly, they can quit education and start work, and this is done by approximately 6 per cent. Secondly, they can attempt to gain entry to an academic senior high school and about two-thirds take this option. The third option, taken by about 30 per cent, is to continue their education in a vocational senior high school or in a technical college.

Of this 30 per cent who opt for a vocationally based education, approximately two-thirds enter vocational senior high schools for a three year course. The remaining third enter the technical colleges for a five year course. These technical colleges were first established in 1962, to increase the technical skills of young people and improve the quality of the labour force. By the 1980s 62 of these technical colleges had been established and there was at least one in every major city. The vocational senior high schools and colleges provide a variety of vocational courses in commercial subjects including book-keeping and shorthand typing, craft skills, electronics, agriculture, fisheries, home economics and nursing.

The social standing of the vocational senior high schools and technical colleges is rather below that of the academic senior high schools, and it tends to be the less academically able adolescents who opt for this form of further education. No doubt many of these adolescents have practical aptitudes whose potential has not been realised up to this point in their educational careers. These schools and colleges have made an important contribution to providing this group of young people with the marketable skills that will secure them employment, and this is undoubtedly an important factor in the low levels of unemployment which have been experienced in Japan, even in the world economic recession of the first half of the 1980s.

In addition to these schools and colleges for technical and vocational education, large and medium sized firms in Japan have their own training schools which provide extensive technical training for their workforce. It is more cost effective for Japanese firms to provide training for their employees than it is in the West because of the Japanese practice of lifetime employment in a single firm. This ensures that the investment a firm makes in providing a thorough training in technical skills for its workforce is rarely wasted by workers leaving and obtaining employment elsewhere.

3.13 UNIVERSITIES

The Japanese universities and colleges of tertiary education are both numerous and of many different kinds. University education has expanded rapidly in Japan since the end of World War Two and by the 1980s some 38 per cent of 18-year-olds proceeded to a university or college. This figure is broadly comparable to that in the United States, and about two or three times that generally prevailing in Britain and

Continental Europe. Japan has 413 universities and 571 colleges as compared with less than 100 universities, polytechnics and other tertiary education establishments in Britain. Thus, the Japanese university and college sector resembles that of the United States more closely than that of Europe in its diversity, numbers and size, the high proportion of young people enrolled and, as described shortly, in its mix of public and private institutions.

Japan does not possess the ancient universities of Europe, or even the seventeenth century foundations such as Harvard in the United States. It was not until 1877 that the University of Tokyo was established as Japan's first university. It was founded by the Japanese government as part of its programme to modernise Japan. The intention was to establish a university which would be the equal of the best in Europe. The university was generously financed and rapidly acquired the high public standing that it has retained to this day.

In succeeding years the Japanese government founded a further six imperial universities in Kyoto, Osaka and other major provincial cities. These are now generally regarded as belonging to the top dozen élite Japanese universities. These were followed in the first half of the present century by the foundation of a number of other public universities.

During the inter-war and post-war period the public demand for university education grew rapidly, and to meet this demand a number of private universities were founded. By the 1980s approximately 80 per cent of Japanese students were enrolled in these private universities and only 20 per cent in the public universities. All universities normally require students to do a four year course for the bachelor's degree, although courses in medicine and dentistry are naturally longer. In addition to the universities there are 571 three year colleges, which although numerous are smaller in size. These colleges are attended by nearly one third of the total number of students. The great majority of the students at these colleges are girls and the subjects they study are principally home economics, the humanities and education, which qualifies them to teach in primary schools. Virtually no science is taught at these colleges. Approximately 90 per cent of the colleges are private and only 10 per cent public.

All universities and colleges in Japan charge fees, but at the public institutions these are quite modest. At the private institutions the fees are generally substantial, although they differ considerably between different institutions and faculties, the fees for science and medicine being higher than those for the humanities and social sciences. Private universities and colleges do however receive some subsidies from government amounting to approximately 15 per cent of their income. The private institutions devote effort to raising endowments and funds and over the sector as a whole succeed in meeting approximately 30 per cent of their running costs from private sources (Ichikawa, 1979). The remaining 55 or so per cent of their costs are met from student fees. There are no grants for students in Japan, but loans are available to enable students to pay the fees and living expenses. These loans are not written off in the case of women students who get married and have children, so that quite a large number of young Japanese women are married with a negative dowry.

Japanese universities and colleges are ranked in a prestige hierarchy in the same way as the senior high schools. In this regard Japanese universities are not of course unique. It has been proposed by Clark (1979) that the university systems in different countries can be viewed according to how sharply they are ordered in a hierarchy of public reputation and esteem. He suggests that in West Germany and Italy all the universities are considered to be more or less equal in status and a hierarchical rank order barely exists. In the United States there is a weak hierarchy. Harvard, Yale, Princeton and Stanford are certainly élite universities; but there are also numerous other highly esteemed universities with only slightly less standing; there are many highly regarded state universities and there are others less highly regarded; there are universities of somewhat lower standing which offer only bachelor's degrees and not doctor's degrees; and there are two year colleges which few have ever heard of outside the localities in which they are situated. Some such status hierarchy of universities and colleges in the United States undoubtedly exists, but it is not particularly strong and the status of the university a person graduates from in the United States has relatively little effect on their subsequent careers.

There are three countries, Clark suggests, which have the most pronounced university hierarchies. The first is France, where the *grandes écoles* established by Napoleon, and especially the Ecole Polytechnique, stand at the apex of the hierarchy and have very high public esteem. The second country is Britain, where the mediaeval foundations of Oxford and Cambridge occupy a similar prestigious position. The third country is Japan.

The prestige hierarchy of universities and colleges in Japan is broadly as follows. The most prestigious university is by common consent the University of Tokyo. Next comes the University of Kyoto, the second oldest university foundation in Japan. There follow some ten or so élite institutions. These comprise the remaining five former Imperial universities and two or three other public universities in Osaka, Kobe, Yokohama and other major provincial cities; also present in this élite group is Hitosubashi, a technological university of high standing resembling the Massachusetts Institute of Technology; and finally there are the two private universities of Waseda and Keio.

Below this top dozen there are some 40 or so universities throughout Japan which command high prestige in their localities but are less well known at the national level. Their position is somewhat akin to that of provincial schools with good local reputations in Britain, such as St Peter's School in York, the King's School in Worcester, King Henry VIII's School in Coventry and so forth, which are well known and respected in their localities but are not in the same class as nationally renowned schools such as Eton or Winchester. In each locality in Japan there are also less highly regarded universities and colleges, and these are ranked in public esteem in terms of their academic reputation and status.

In general the public universities have higher reputations in Japan than the private universities. It has been noted that only the two private universities of Waseda and Keio are considered as belonging to the top dozen universities in Japan, and it is the public universities which also figure predominantly among the next 40 or so prestigious universities. The Japanese public universities are quite generously financed by government and hence can afford the kind of facilities enjoyed by universities in Britain or the major universities in the United States. The private universities in Japan, being heavily reliant on income from fees, have in general found it impossible to match the facilities of the public universities and are therefore usually regarded as second-best institutions.

The public universities in Japan are highly meritocratic in the sense that entry is secured on merit and not by the purse. The public universities charge only modest fees, loans are available for fees and living expenses and many students live quite cheaply at home, so that these élite and prestigious universities are open in principle, and to a considerable extent in practice, to all who are sufficiently talented to secure entry to them. In this respect Japan resembles Britain, where the public grants for students enable all able young people to go to Oxford or Cambridge if they can pass the entrance examinations. The United States differs from Japan and Britain in this regard because the most prestigious universities are in general the private Ivy League and similar foundations, from which many talented young Americans are debarred from access by the high fees. These financial constraints have the effect that the most talented young Americans are more widely spread over numerous American universities, whereas in Japan and Britain they are more concentrated in the élite universities. This is one of the major reasons for the higher prestige of the Japanese and British élite universities and the flatter prestige hierarchy of universities in the United States.

In addition to meritocratic entry, the high prestige of the University of Tokyo and the other élite Japanese universities is sustained, like that of the *grandes écoles* in France and of Oxford and Cambridge in Britain, by a kind of benign (or vicious, according to viewpoint) circle. The prestige of these universities has the effect that entry is highly desired and competitive and they are able to select very able and ambitious young men (nearly all the students are male). These young men generally do well in their careers and in due course come to occupy many of the top positions in Japanese society. The extent of the hold of graduates from the University of Tokyo alone on top positions in Japan strikes many Western observers as remarkable. Over the last three decades half of Japan's prime ministers have been Tokyo university graduates. Surveys have shown that Tokyo graduates occupy approximately two-thirds of the most senior positions in the civil service, and one third of those in the major corporations (Rohlen, 1983). The same hold of Tokyo graduates is also present in the top positions of the legal and medical professions.

Where the top positions in the Japanese civil service, industry and professions are not held by Tokyo graduates, they are largely held by graduates of the dozen or so other élite universities. To a considerable extent the reason for this is that these institutions recruit their graduate intakes largely and often exclusively from these universities. Those responsible for recruiting graduate trainees for future senior management take the view that if young men are sufficiently intelligent, ambitious and organised to obtain entry to Tokyo or one of the other élite universities, they are likely to have the right qualities for success in their organisations.

Middle-sized Japanese firms recruit their intakes from less highly regarded universities in the middle ranges of the status hierarchy. The Japanese have a tradition of lifelong employment in a single company. There is no developed labour market for executives in mid-career to switch from one company to another as there is in Europe and the United States. The effect of this is that the standing of the university attended is a crucial determinant of an individual's future career in Japan.

The powerful hold of graduates from Tokyo and the dozen élite universities on senior positions in Japan receives widespread publicity in the Japanese media. The public is consequently well aware that to achieve success in the major avenues of Japanese society it is almost mandatory to graduate from one of these universities. The incentive for young Japanese adolescents to secure entry to one of these universities is therefore very powerful. It is certainly far stronger than the corresponding incentive for adolescents in the United States, where no-one believes that to succeed in the major American career structures it is virtually essential to graduate from Harvard or from one of a small group of other prestigious colleges. This is undoubtedly one of the major reasons why Japanese adolescents work so much harder at school than American adolescents. Given the structure of Japanese universities and careers, they are entirely realistic to do so.

3.14 CONCLUSIONS

The objective of this chapter has been to present an outline of the major features of Japanese education. Although the account given has been primarily descriptive, it should be possible to discern some of the major causal factors involved in the high educational standards achieved by Japanese school children. Educational achievement can be considered broadly as a product of three classes of input, namely the characteristics of children, of their parents, and of their teachers.

(a) Characteristics of Japanese Children

We have suggestive evidence that Japanese children are strongly motivated for academic work. During the teenage years approximately half of Japanese children attend the supplementary coaching schools known as the *juku* during the evenings, at weekends and during the school holidays. It is an interesting question why similar extramural coaching schools have not been established in Britain, the United States and Continental Europe. The answer to this must surely be that neither parents nor their children are sufficiently motivated to make use of such schools. If the demand were present, it would surely have been met by enterprising educational entrepreneurs and such schools would have been established.

A second indication of the strong educational motivation of Japanese children is the high percentage who continue their education voluntarily beyond the minimum legal school leaving age. No less than 94 per cent of Japanese adolescents in the 15–18 age range group pursue their education voluntarily in schools or colleges. In Britain only approximately 50 per cent of 16-year-olds are prepared to continue their education beyond the legally permitted school leaving age. In France and West Germany approximately 65 per cent of young people in late adolescence continue their education voluntarily. In the United States approximately 80 per cent of 18-year-olds graduate from high school. The 94 per cent who continue their education voluntarily in Japan must surely be attributed to the high motivation for educational achievement among Japanese adolescents.

This strong motivation is again evident in the high proportion of Japanese 18 to 22-year-olds who continue their education at the tertiary level. The following figures are given by Hayes, Anderson and Fonda (1984, p. 82) for the percentages of the 18 to 22-year-olds who gained tertiary education qualifications in universities or colleges in the years 1979–1981:

Japan	37	United Kingdom	14
United States	32	West Germany	8

Thus even in the affluent United States fewer young people acquire tertiary education qualifications than in Japan. The contrast between Japan and Britain in this regard is more striking, because in Britain tertiary education is free and students receive relatively generous financial support from governments in the form of grants. In spite of this, there are unfilled places in British universities and polytechnics. One of the major reasons for these unfilled places is that not enough young people in Britain are sufficiently motivated to do the academic work necessary to gain the entrance requirements for admission. In Japan young people have to pay their own way through university, and yet many more of them are prepared to do so than in Britain. The fact that so many young Japanese are willing to pay for their university or college education is further testimony to the strong motivation for education among young people in Japan.

The reasons for the high level of motivation for educational achievement among young Japanese are complex, and are the subject of analysis in later chapters. Nevertheless, two factors stand out and are noted at this stage. Firstly, the 'fourteen plus' examinations taken by nearly all young Japanese for entry to hierarchically ranked senior high schools act as a powerful motivator for academic work. These examinations have a backwash effect on the 12–14 year age group. The hope of doing well, and the fear of doing poorly, in these examinations are certainly an important factor in the motivation for academic work among Japanese teenagers. There are no corresponding incentives of this strength in the West.

Secondly, once Japanese 15-year-olds have found places in their senior high schools their motivation for academic work is sustained by the wish to do well in the seventeen and eighteen plus examinations for entry into hierarchically ranked universities. Japanese adolescents perceive that as graduates of a prestigious university they will acquire both social standing and enhanced job prospects, and they are motivated to work hard to achieve this objective.

While it may be objected that the hope of securing entry to a prestigious university fulfils an incentive function for adolescents to do academic work in many countries, the incentive effect is uniquely powerful in Japan. There are three reasons for this. Firstly, the status attached to being a graduate of the University of Tokyo or of one of the dozen or so élite universities, or failing those one of 40 or so other prestigious universities, is very high in Japan. Secondly, compared with Europe, there are two or three times as many young people entering higher education in Japan, so that a substantially greater proportion are exposed to the motivating effects of attempting to obtain entry to a university of high standing. Compared with the United States, broadly similar proportions of young people enter tertiary education as in Japan, but the credential value of graduation from a prestigious university is not so great in the United States.

A third factor which enhances the incentive effects of the Japanese university entrance examinations is the practice of Japanese firms and the civil service of recruiting graduate trainees for senior management from the prestigious universities, and then providing them with lifelong employment. This tradition makes securing entry to a prestigious university a crucially important step on the ladder of a successful career, and is an important element in the motivational effect of the hierarchically structured Japanese universities on the academic work effort of adolescents.

(b) Characteristics of Japanese Parents

The second important input for educational achievement lies in the attitudes of parents and the value they attach to education. These parental attitudes and values are transmitted to children by subtle psychological processes which are analysed later. For the present we can note some preliminary indications that Japanese parents attach considerable importance to their children's educational achievement. Firstly, approximately 80 per cent of Japanese pre-school children are sent to kindergarten, as compared with approximately 40 per cent in Britain and the United States. Three-quarters of the kindergarten in Japan are private fee paying establishments. It is evident therefore that a far greater proportion of Japanese parents are willing to make financial sacrifices to give their young children an early start in their educational career than is the case in Britain and the United States. It cannot be objected that sufficient kindergarten do not exist in Britain and the United States, for surely if significantly greater demand were present among parents more kindergarten would be established as private fee paying schools.

The willingness of Japanese parents to devote their own financial resources to further their children's education is again evident in the teenage years, when approximately half of Japanese parents pay for their children to attend the supplementary evening and holiday *juku*. At the senior high school stage 30 per cent of Japanese parents pay quite appreciable fees for their teenage children's education, and at the university 80 per cent of students have to pay substantial fees which are met from family resources as well as from loans. In all these ways the willingness of such large numbers of Japanese parents to make financial sacrifices to further their children's education suggests a commitment to educational achievement which is stronger and more widely diffused among the population than is the case in the West.

(c) Characteristics of Japanese Teachers

The third input determining the educational standards of school children is the professionalism of teachers. We have not seen any direct evidence bearing on the degree of professionalism of Japanese teachers. This again will be considered later. Nevertheless, at this stage it is noted that the competitive relationship between the senior high schools in Japan is likely to generate a higher level of commitment among teachers than is generally present in the West. A description has been given of the way these schools are ranked annually in Japan on the basis of the educational attainments of their pupils, the publicity given to these annual rankings by the media and the widespread interest taken in them by the Japanese public. The result of this is that the educational efficiency or otherwise of the senior high schools has very high visibility in Japan. The psychological effect of this on Japanese teachers is that teachers' feelings of self-esteem become bound up with the academic achievements of their schools, and this acts as a source of motivation to teach efficiently in order to maintain and enhance the schools' academic reputations.

The largely descriptive account of the Japanese education system given in this chapter has suggested some, but not all, of the major factors responsible for the high educational standards which prevail in Japan. We turn now to a more analytic account of these factors and consider first an important determinant of educational achievement which we have as yet barely noticed, namely the intelligence of Japanese children.

4 The Intelligence of Japanese Children

Intelligence is a major determinant of educational achievement and it is therefore natural to ask whether the high educational standards of Japanese children may be due to superior intelligence. The term intelligence is used in the sense of an individual's general learning and problem solving abilities. It is generally considered that these abilities are acquired through both inherited and environmental determinants and are adequately measured by intelligence tests (see, for example, Eysenck, 1979; Vernon, 1979; Jensen, 1980).

4.1 INTELLIGENCE AND EDUCATIONAL ACHIEVEMENT

It has been found in numerous studies that intelligence is highly associated with educational achievement. In a review of a number of investigations in the United States, Parkerson, Schiller, Lomax and Walberg (1984) conclude that the correlations between the two are typically in the range of 0.6 to 0.7. In one of our own studies of the determinants of educational achievement among approximately 700 adolescents in a small town in Northern Ireland, we found that an intelligence test administered in the early autumn correlated 0.64 with educational achievement as measured by performance on GCE 'O' level and CSE examinations taken approximately six months later (Lynn, Hampson and Magee, 1983). The intelligence of a child can be measured with relative reliability at the ages of three or four years and is predictive of educational achievement many years later (see, for example, Eysenck, 1979). For this reason it is generally considered that intelligence is causal to subsequent educational achievement.

4.2 NON-VERBAL TESTS OF JAPANESE INTELLIGENCE

The intelligence of Japanese children has been the subject of a number of studies from the mid-1970s onwards. The initial studies compared the performance of Japanese and American children on American non-verbal intelligence tests. These non-verbal tests involve problems presented in the form of pictures, diagrams, blocks and so forth. It is more straightforward to administer tests of this kind from one country to another because there are none of the translation problems which are involved with verbal tests. Furthermore, it is widely held that non-verbal tests give a truer measure of underlying ability, or what Cattell (1971) has called 'fluid intelligence', because they are less affected by environmental conditions than verbal tests.

Several of these investigations involving the administration of American non-verbal intelligence tests to Japanese children have found that Japanese children obtained significantly higher mean IQs than those in the United States. The highest figure reported for the Japanese IQ is that of Hilger, Klett and Watson (1976), who used a drawing test of intelligence and found a mean IQ of 138 for Japanese children from a village in the northern island of Hokkaido. This figure is so high that some doubt will probably be entertained as to whether it can be a valid measure of Japanese intelligence. Nevertheless, mean IQs of 111 and 113 were obtained for Japanese children from the Japanese standardisations of the performance scales of the Wechsler tests (Lynn, 1977, 1982a), and Misawa, Motegi, Fujita and Hattori (1984) obtained a mean Japanese IQ of 113 from the standardisation in Japan of the Columbia Mental Maturity Scale, a non-verbal reasoning test. These results appeared to suggest that the mean IQ of Japanese children is significantly higher than that of American children, and also than that of children in Britain and Continental Europe, since these have approximately the same mean IQ as American children (Lynn, 1977).

These results provoked a certain amount of controversy and it has become clear that they need qualification in several important respects. Firstly, it has only recently become evident that intelligence is increasing at quite a rapid rate in the economically advanced nations. The rate of increase in Britain, Japan and the United States is approximately 3 IQ points per decade (Flynn, 1984; Lynn and Hampson, 1986d). Since in the Japanese–American comparisons the Japanese tests were given later than the American, an adjustment has to be made for this time interval and this reduces the Japanese lead. Secondly, approximately 15 per cent of American children are black. The low mean IQ of these reduces the American mean by 1.7 IQ points and a further adjustment for this needs to be made for a comparison between Japanese children and white American children. Taken together, these two adjustments have the effect of reducing the Japanese mean IQ in the studies cited above by around 2.5 to 3.0 IQ points. This is a relatively minor adjustment and still leaves the mean Japanese IQ substantially above that of white American (and European) children.

A third qualification that needs consideration is the possibility that the samples of children used for the standardisation of the tests in Japan may have been biased in favour of more intelligent children, and therefore have yielded spuriously high mean IQs. This criticism has been made by Stevenson and Azuma (1983) of the Wechsler (WISC-R) results. These critics maintain that 92 per cent of the children in the Japanese standardisation sample come from towns or cities with populations greater than 50 000, whereas only 64 per cent of the population of Japan resides in towns and cities of this size. They point out that urban children tend to have somewhat higher intelligence than country children in Japan, as they do elsewhere. This criticism has been answered by Motegi (1984), one of the Japanese psychologists responsible for the Japanese standardisation of this test. He defends the sampling largely on the grounds that 98.5 per cent of the Japanese population live in towns of more than 5000 inhabitants. Hence virtually the whole population are urban dwellers and stratified sampling for the size of the town or city is unnecessary. This seems a satisfactory answer. Even more telling, however, is the fact that so many investigations yield the same conclusion, to the effect that the mean Japanese IQ measured by non-verbal tests is higher than that of white American children by somewhere between one half and two-thirds of a standard deviation. It is difficult to believe that different Japanese psychologists responsible for these standardisations of these different tests would have all drawn samples biased upwards. It is therefore believed that this Japanese superiority is genuine, although it is not the whole story.

4.3 THE PATTERN OF JAPANESE ABILITIES

The studies reviewed in the preceding section treated intelligence as a single entity measured by the IQ, and assumed that the Japanese IQ has been adequately assessed by non-verbal intelligence tests. As a result of further work it has become clear that this view is fallacious, and a more sophisticated analysis of Japanese intelligence is given in this section.

The leading model of intelligence is the hierarchial model first advanced by Burt (1949) and Vernon (1950). This model conceptualises intelligence as a hierarchical pyramid of abilities. At the apex stands general intelligence, first identified by Spearman and known as Spearman's *g*. This general ability is applied to all cognitive tasks and is an important determinant of the efficiency with which they are performed. Spearman's *g* can be split into two further abilities known as the group verbal and the group visuospatial abilities. These two group abilities can each be split down further into some ten to fifteen primary abilities which stand at the foot of the hierarchical pyramid. Thus group verbal ability can be split into verbal comprehension, verbal memory span, numerical ability, word fluency, etc., and group visuospatial ability into spatial and perceptual abilities of various kinds and drawing ability. This model commands widespread acceptance among leading contemporary workers on intelligence (see, for example, Eysenck, 1979; Vernon, 1979; Jensen, 1980).

If this model is applied to the problem of the intelligence of the Japanese it will be clear that we can obtain a much more sophisticated analysis than was given by the initial studies using the non-verbal tests. These tests provided measures of the Japanese group visuospatial factor or of some of the narrower primary abilities of which this factor is composed, such as drawing ability. It was assumed that these were adequate measures of Spearman's *g*, but this is not necessarily the case. Considered in terms of the hierarchical model, it is clear that what is required for a fuller description of Japanese intelligence are more accurate measures of Spearman's *g* and of the group verbal factor, as well as the group visuospatial factor.

We have made three studies of this problem using the Japanese standardisations of three American intelligence tests which are suitable for this purpose. These are the McCarthy Scales of Children's Abilities covering the ages from 2½ to 8 years, the Wechsler Pre-school and Primary Scale for Intelligence covering the ages from 4 to 6, and the Wechsler Intelligence Scale for Children covering the ages from 6 to 16. The technical details of the quantification of Japanese abilities in terms of the hierarchical model have been given in journal articles, to which the interested reader is referred (Lynn and Hampson, 1986a, b and c). What is given here is a summary of the results.

The values for the leading abilities in the hierarchical model for Japanese children over the age range 2 to 16 years are set out in Table 4.1. These Japanese abilities are calculated in relation to a mean of 100 and a standard deviation of 15 for white American children. They are also adjusted for the time lags of three or four years between the American and Japanese standardisations and they relate approximately to the year 1975. Japanese values for Spearman's *g* and the

Table 4.1   Mean IQs of Japanese children in relation to white American means of 100 and standard deviation of 15

Age	Spearman's g	Verbal GF	Visuospatial GF	Age	Spearman's g	Verbal GF	Visuospatial GF
2½	94.4	92.8	97.0	8	99.9	95.3	105.6
3	94.1	92.5	96.5	9	102.3	99.0	105.8
3½	96.6	94.7	99.5	10	104.1	101.0	106.5
4	95.9	93.1	99.6	11	104.0	100.7	106.2
4½	97.1	93.8	101.6	12	104.4	100.9	106.1
5	97.2	92.6	103.7	13	103.4	100.3	104.8
5½	98.7	93.8	105.7	14	104.0	100.8	105.4
6	101.0	97.0	105.7	15	104.2	101.3	105.4
7	99.2	94.7	105.4	16	103.3	100.8	103.0

For ages 6–16, deviations of 3.6 and 4.7 from 100 are statistically significant at the .05 and .01 per cent levels. For ages 2–5, deviations of 5.1 and 6.7 from 100 are statistically significant at the .05 and .01 per cent levels
Source: Lynn (1987)

group verbal and group visuospatial factors have been calculated from factor scores derived from factor analyses of the scores of the individual tests. Where there is overlap in the ages covered by the three tests (for example, all three tests give scores for 6-year-olds) the scores have been averaged in the results set out in Table 4.1.

The principal features of interest in this table are as follows. In the first column are given Japanese values for Spearman's g. At the age of 2 years Japanese infants obtain a mean IQ of 94.4, and this is significantly lower than the mean of 100 of white American infants. From the ages of three years onwards it appears that Japanese children's values for Spearman's g steadily improve.

Between the age of 3½ and 9 years there are no significant differences between Japanese and white American children, while from the age of 10 years upwards Japanese children obtain higher means on Spearman's g. Looking at the age trends of Japanese children, it is clear that they start with lower general intelligence than American children, gradually catch up and then surpass American children from the age of 10 years.

There are two possible explanations for this developmental trend. The first is that Japanese children are genetically inferior for Spearman's g but have an exceptionally favourable environment which is responsible for the steady improvement in their intelligence. The second explanation is that Japanese children are genetically programmed slow maturers up to the age of about six years. By this age they are approximately the equal of American children. It is considered that this is the preferable explanation. The superiority of Japanese children from the age of ten years onwards should probably be attributed largely to the more favourable environment of Japanese children.

Looking now at the group verbal and group visuospatial abilities set out in columns two and three of Table 4.1, it will be seen that in both of these Japanese children show the same initial weaknesses followed by gradual improvement. It is considered that these trends are further expressions of the slow maturation of Japanese children. During the school years the verbal abilities improve from about 96 at ages 6 to 7 to about 101 at ages 10 to 16. This improvement should probably be attributable largely to the superior efficiency of Japanese schools. The verbal abilities, such as vocabulary, verbal comprehension, arithmetic and so forth, are taught in schools, while the visuospatial abilities are not taught. Hence the visuospatial abilities of Japanese children do not display the steady increase over the school years that occurs in the case of the verbal abilities.

It will be clear from the IQs set out in Table 4.1 that Japanese children have a highly distinctive pattern of intelligence. The most striking features are the weak verbal abilities and the strong visuospatial abilities. It is difficult to envisage a set of environmental conditions which could have the effect of depressing the verbal abilities and at the same time enhancing the visuospatial abilities. It is considered therefore that this pattern of abilities in Japanese children probably has some genetic basis. This problem is not of immediate relevance to Japanese educational achievement and has been discussed elsewhere for readers who wish to pursue it (Lynn, 1987). Our concern is with the contribution of this pattern of abilities, however caused, to the educational achievement of Japanese children.

4.4 CONTRIBUTION OF JAPANESE INTELLIGENCE TO EDUCATIONAL ACHIEVEMENT

In considering the question of the relevance of the distinctive pattern of Japanese abilities to Japanese educational achievement it is useful to distinguish the primary school from the secondary school stages. At the primary stage school work is principally determined by general intelligence and the group verbal factor, and relatively little by the group visuospatial factor. Thus, in a study of Japanese 11-year-old children, it has been found by Kashiwagi, Azuma and Miyake (1982) that the verbal IQ of the Wechsler (WISC-R) test was correlated 0.58 with a composite score of educational achievement consisting of arithmetic, language, social studies and science, while the Wechsler non-verbal IQ (essentially a measure of the group visuospatial factor) correlated only 0.29 with educational achievement. The reason for the higher association of the group verbal factor than of the group visuospatial factor with educational achievement at the primary school stage is that school learning at this age is largely a matter of proficiency in reading, verbal learning and memorisation. This includes arithmetic, which numerous studies have shown belongs to the group verbal factor (see, for example, Blaha and Wallbrown, 1984).

It would therefore be expected that since Japanese children are weak on the group verbal factor they would do relatively poorly on tests of reading and arithmetic at the primary school stage. The chief source of evidence on this question is the Minneapolis-Sendai study carried out by Stigler, Lee, Lucker and Stevenson (1982) and summarised in Chapter 2. It will be recalled that Japanese 10-year-olds do perform at a lower average standard on reading vocabulary compared with American children. This follows naturally from the relatively poor verbal abilities of Japanese children.

On the other hand, Japanese 6-year-olds and 10-year-olds do better in arithmetic than American children. This result is paradoxical because arithmetical skills are partly determined by the group verbal factor. The most straightforward explanation for the strong arithmetical ability of Japanese children is that the arithmetic skills are so efficiently taught in Japanese schools. In general Japanese children are at a disadvantage at the stage of primary school education by virtue of their poor verbal abilities, but these are overcome in arithmetic by efficient teaching.

At the secondary school stage the picture is somewhat different. At this stage the group visuospatial factor and the spatial primary begin to contribute to educational achievement in subjects like physics and some branches of mathematics. Both French (1964) and Fennema and Sherman (1977) have found correlations of 0.4 between spatial ability and achievement in mathematics and physics. The reason for the positive associations between the visuospatial abilities and achievement in mathematics and physics is that a number of problems in these subjects can be tackled visually. This is particularly the case with geometry and mechanics. It is evident therefore that Japanese children, with their higher visuospatial abilities, are likely to have some advantage over Western children for certain problems in secondary school mathematics and physics.

On the other hand, there is no doubt that many problems in mathematics and science generally can also be solved by the verbal abilities. There has been a good deal of recent work on this question in connection with the problem of why adolescent boys tend to be superior on average to girls in mathematics. The upshot of this research is that both verbal and visuospatial abilities are used for tackling problems in mathematics and that those with strong verbal skills (predominantly girls) use these for tackling mathematical problems, while those with strong visuospatial skills (predominantly boys) employ these (Aiken, 1971; Chipman, Brush and Wilson, 1985; Fennema and Tartre, 1985). The conclusion of these researchers is that neither the verbal nor the visuospatial abilities confers any unique advantages for achievement in mathematics. If this is the case, it follows that the high visuospatial abilities of Japanese adolescents does not give them any particular advantage in mathematics or, probably, science in general, since Western adolescents have a complementary advantage in being able to apply their higher verbal abilities to these subjects.

4.5. CONCLUSIONS

Although intelligence is an important determinant of educational achievement for individual children in all countries, it does not appear to be a significant factor in the high educational standards in Japan. The most important ability for educational achievement is Spearman's g. There are no differences in this ability between Japanese and white American children over the age range 6 to 9 years. Japanese children do show some superiority on Spearman's g from the age of ten years onwards, but a superiority of around 4 IQ points would not make much contribution to their higher educational achievement, and in any case this superiority is probably largely an effect of the efficiency of Japanese schools.

The verbal and visuospatial group ability factors also affect educational achievement. The Japanese have a distinctive pattern of these consisting of weak verbal ability and strong visuospatial ability. At the primary school stage the verbal abilities are more important. Hence Japanese children are handicapped, but in arithmetic this handicap is overcome by efficient teaching and the net result is that Japanese arithmetical skills are raised to a higher level than those in the United States.

At the secondary school stage the visuospatial abilities assume greater importance for educational achievement in some branches of mathematics and science. Here the strong visuospatial abilities of Japanese adolescents will be useful, but Western adolescents are the equal of Japanese on the verbal abilities and can use these for the solution of mathematical and scientific problems. Nevertheless, Japanese adolescents will have some advantage over Western adolescents by virtue of their higher Spearman's g and their strong visuospatial abilities. This advantage will, however, be relatively small, accounting for around one-tenth of the superior educational standards of Japanese adolescents. For an understanding of the major factors determining the high educational achievement of Japanese adolescents we must look elsewhere, and especially at motivation and incentives.

5 Motivation and Incentives for Educational Achievement in Japan and the West

Motivation is an important determinant of educational achievement. A review of 40 studies of the effects of school children's motivation has been published by Parkerson, Schiller, Lomax and Walberg (1984), in which they found a median correlation of 0.34 between motivation and educational achievement. The possible contribution of motivation in the educational standards of Japanese school children is the subject of this chapter.

Students of motivation distinguish two kinds of motivation which are normally designated *extrinsic* and *intrinsic*. Extrinsic motivation is generated by external or extrinsic incentives. For instance, a child may be offered a sweet for doing a sum and getting the correct answer. In these circumstances the sweet serves as an incentive and generates motivation to expend the effort necessary to secure it. Sweets and other desirable objects are known in psychology as rewards or reinforcements. There is also negative extrinsic motivation, which is generated by the anticipation of punishment. The child may be informed that not doing the sum will be followed by punishment and this also generates motivation to expend work effort to avoid the threatened punishment.

Extrinsic motivation is essentially a reformation in contemporary terminology of Jeremy Bentham's thesis of the hedonic calculus, which he set out in the late eighteenth century in his *Introduction to the Principles of Morals and Legislation* (Bentham, 1789). In this book Bentham proposed that human beings pursue pleasure and avoid pain and that their behaviour is motivated, positively or negatively, by the anticipated pleasurable or painful consequences to which they believe their actions will lead. This proposition became the foundation of the theories of motivation which were developed in the academic disciplines of both economics and psychology. In economics it was expressed as the principle of the maximisation of utility and in psychology as the maximisation of reinforcement. A useful discussion

61

and summary of the essential similarities in the formulations of these theories of motivation in economics and psychology has been presented by Rachlin, Battalio, Kagel and Green (1981).

It is clear that this theory captures many important aspects of human motivation. For instance, positive incentives largely determine the degree to which people will work for money and it has been shown in numerous investigations that the amount of work effort which people expend varies with the strength of the financial incentives available (see, for example, Vroom, 1964; Staw, 1977). Similarly, the negative incentives of the anticipation of punishment play an important part in people's respect for the criminal law (see, for example, Wilson and Herrnstein, 1985).

Nevertheless, in psychology, although not to any significant extent in economics, it is appreciated that there is more to motivation than the anticipation of reinforcing or punishing incentives. There is also intrinsic motivation. This is the motivation to work in order to satisfy some internal standard or value such as a moral conviction that work ought to be done and done properly and that laziness is wicked. Intrinsic motivations of this and similar kinds are certainly as important as extrinsic motivations. They are, however, set aside for consideration in the next chapter. In the present chapter we discuss only extrinsic motivation and its contribution to Japanese educational achievement. We consider first the general question of the effects of incentives on academic work, secondly the incentives for school children in Japan, and finally, those available for school children in Britain, the United States and Continental Europe.

5.1 INCENTIVES AND EDUCATIONAL ACHIEVEMENT

In general terms the idea that children respond to incentives is common sense. Teachers have made use of incentives for many centuries, employing marks, stars, prizes, grades and so forth as incentives for good work and various punishments, including low marks, as negative incentives or punishments for poor work.

In the post-World War Two period the effects of incentives have been more systematically studied in the context of learning in schools and other educational settings. A variety of incentives have been used, including sweets for young children, tokens exchangeable for sweets or toys, and grades or marks. The classical study of the motivating effects of tests on the basis of which grades were awarded was undertaken during the Second World War. Soldiers were being taught the military phonetic alphabet (A-able; B-baker, etc.) and different conditions of learning were investigated. The results showed that when tests were given and grades awarded, the learning was better. This appears to be the first empirical demonstration, using appropriate control groups, that tests and grades act as incentives, enhance motivation and improve performance (Hovland, Lumsdaine and Sheffield, 1949). Several other studies of this kind showing the same effects are reviewed by Berliner (1985).

So far as young children are concerned, some of the first studies to demonstrate the advantageous effects of incentives were carried out by Staats and his colleagues. Their work consisted of giving children tokens as reinforcements for learning. The tokens served as a form of money and could be exchanged for sweets and toys. These experiments were carried out on 4-year-olds and demonstrated that these young children both learned to read and would read for prolonged periods of time when reinforced in this way (Staats, Staats, Schutz and Wolf, 1962; Staats, Finley, Minke, Wolf and Brooks, 1964).

Following this initial work a large number of further studies have been published on the effectiveness of tokens given as reinforcements for various classroom, behaviours which the investigators have wished to encourage. It has been found that four broad classes of behaviour can be increased through the administration of tokens as reinforcements. These are persistence in study, attention to the task with concomitant decreases in disruptive behaviour, attendance at lessons as opposed to truancy, and learning. Much of the quite extensive work on the effectiveness of tokens given as reinforcements for academic work has been reviewed by O'Leary and Drabman (1971) and Hayes (1976). These studies have established beyond doubt that such reinforcements enhance children's academic motivation and achievement.

A further body of work has shown that grades and marks also act as reinforcements and motivators for children's academic work and achievement. This work is reviewed by Michaels (1977), Slavin, (1977) and Johnson, Maruyama, Johnson, Nelson and Skon (1981). Here the grades or marks cannot be exchanged for toys, sweets or money, as is the case with tokens, but nevertheless apparently act as reinforcements and incentives. It is normally assumed that grades or marks exert their reinforcing effect because they reward children's needs for self-esteem and competitive success, and that these needs are as strong, if not stronger, than the needs for sweets and toys.

There is therefore a considerable body of work in educational psychology to show that where academic achievement among children is rewarded it acquires incentive value. In these conditions children readily learn that reinforcements are contingent on work effort and they will expend the work effort necessary to secure the proferred reinforcements.

5.2 MOTIVATION OF JAPANESE SCHOOL CHILDREN

There is little doubt that Japanese school children are strongly motivated for academic work and that this motivation plays a significant part in their high educational standards. Many observers of the educational scene in Japan have testified to the strong motivation for academic work among Japanese school schildren. Cummings (1980) contrasts the disorder prevalent in the typical American high school, where teachers struggle to maintain discipline, with the 'sobriety' and quiet earnestness of high schools in Japan. Similar observations have been made by Rohlen (1983).

In addition to the testimony of observers, the strong motivation of Japanese school children is evident from their behaviour. Far more Japanese children do school work voluntarily than is the case in the West. There are three principal areas in which this voluntary work is undertaken. Firstly, 94 per cent of Japanese adolescents continue their education voluntarily beyond the statutory school leaving age. In Britain only approximately 48 per cent do so and even in the United States the figure is only 80 per cent. Secondly, approximately half of Japanese children voluntarily attend the supplementary schools known as *juku*.

Thirdly, Japanese school children do substantially more homework than is typically undertaken by children in the West. At primary school Japanese children do about 50 per cent more homework than American children (Stigler, Lee, Lucker and Stevenson, 1982), although among this age group it may be argued that this reflects coercion by teachers and parents more than high motivation in the child. However, among 16- to 18-year-olds it is estimated by Walberg *et al.* (1985) that Japanese adolescents do approximately 60 hours of homework per week as compared with 5 hours done by American adolescents. It is difficult to believe that coercive pressures alone could achieve this amount of dedication to homework. The reason that Japanese adolescents work so hard must be that they are highly motivated to do so. It is not easy to distinguish the degree to which this motivation is extrinsic or intrinsic. Comparative studies of Japanese and Western adolescents using questionnaires to measure various forms of intrinsic motivation make it clear that this is a component in the total work motivation of Japanese adolescents. These studies are reviewed in the next chapter where intrinsic motivation is considered. But the way in which Japanese adolescents so universally refer to this stage of their lives as 'examination hell' clearly suggests that their intensive school work is not entirely a labour of love, and that a significant proportion of their motivation is extrinsic, that is purely a function of the external incentives for work effort.

5.3 INCENTIVES IN JAPANESE EDUCATION

The reason why the extrinsic motivation of Japanese school children is so strong lies in the strength of the incentives for educational achievement in Japan. The key to the understanding of the strong motivation of Japanese school children is to be found in an examination of the incentives for educational achievement in the Japanese school system. There are two particularly powerful incentives for educational achievement in Japan. The first confronts Japanese school children at the age of fourteen and consists of the entrance examinations taken by virtually all Japanese children for entry to senior high schools. We have described in Chapter 3 how in every locality in Japan the senior high schools are ranked in public esteem. Japanese school children are well aware that securing entry to a prestigious senior high school will both confer status for life, somewhat akin to that of the 'old school tie' in England, and also be an important first step on the ladder to a prestigious university and career. An important feature of these 'fourteen plus' entrance examinations for senior high school is that they provide incentives for the great majority of Japanese school children, and not merely for the most able. The existence of these 'fourteen plus' examinations inevitably exerts a backwash effect on the preceding two or three years, and is undoubtedly one of the most important reasons that the educational standards of Japanese 13- and 14-year-olds are so high.

The second important incentive for many Japanese adolescents comes three years later and consists of the university entrance examinations. Once Japanese 14- to 15-year-olds have secured admission to their various senior high schools, they are confronted in three years' time with a further set of examinations for entry to universities and colleges, which are again hierarchically ranked in public esteem. A description of the status ranking of Japanese universities has been given in Chapter 3. It will be recalled that the University of Tokyo stands at the apex of this system, followed by a dozen or so highly prestigious universities, a further 40 or so well regarded provincial universities, and below these by a variety of local colleges. The graded hierarchy of the universities mirrors that of the senior high schools.

The hierarchical ranking of universities in public esteem in Japan exerts unusually powerful incentive effects on adolescents for academic work for two principal reasons. The first is that so many more adolescents aspire to university education than in the West, with the exception of the United States. Approximately 38 per cent of young Japanese go to university or college, two or three times the number in Britain and Continental Europe. Hence the incentive effect of the university entrance examinations in raising the academic standards of adolescents acts on a considerably greater proportion of the age group.

The second reason why the incentive effect of these examinations is so powerful lies in the exceptionally high value in Japan of graduation from a high status university. Major Japanese companies and the civil service recruit their trainees for senior manangement almost exclusively from the élite universities, and once these trainees are appointed they normally stay throughout their working lives in the same institution. Japanese professionals do not move from one company to another in mid-career to anything like the extent that they do in the West. It is this practice of the lifelong employment in the same company that makes the standing of the university from which an individual graduates far more important for the whole course of his future career than is the case in Britain, the United States or Continental Europe.

The effects of this system are not merely felt by a small number of the most able who aspire to obtain entry to the élite universities. Middle-sized and smaller companies recruit their management trainees from universities of more moderate standing, so that there is an incentive for adolescents of more modest abilities to attempt to gain entry to these middle ranking universities. These incentive effects of university entrance examinations on the academic work effort of adolescents in the 16- to 18-year-old age range are of course also present to varying degrees in the Western nations, but the sheer number of young people affected in Japan and the very high credential value attached to the university attended make the university entrance examinations more crucial events for future careers in Japan than in the West. In the context of Japanese society and conventions it is not at all difficult to understand why Japanese adolescents work as hard as they do.

5.4 THREE PARAMETERS OF INCENTIVES FOR WORK MOTIVATION

It has been seen that in broad terms the Japanese educational system provides two powerful incentives for academic work in the form of the 'fourteen plus' examinations for entry to senior high schools and the university entrance examinations for universities hierarchically ranked in public esteem. In this section we consider in more detail three parameters of effective incentives and describe how these operate in Japanese education.

A term commonly employed in the psychology of incentives is that of *goal*. To set individuals goals is to provide them with incentives. Research in this field has established three properties of goals which are particularly important for them to function well as incentives. These are that they should be specific rather than general, that they should be ordered in a temporal sequence of sub-goals, and that they should be challenging. In this section we examine these three parameters and the way in which the Japanese educational system fulfils the requirements of effective goals.

(a) Effects of Setting Specific Goals

People in positions of authority frequently set goals for those whose efforts they are attempting to direct. For instance, sales managers set salesmen the goal of selling a certain quantity of goods or services; or a teacher may set children the goal of doing a certain piece of homework. These goals can be of varying degrees of generality or specificity. The sales manager or the teacher may set a general goal to 'do as well as you can'; alternatively, they may set specific and quantified goals such as, in the case of a sales manager, to sell a given volume of goods or, in the case of a teacher, to learn a specified amount of material.

Research in this area has shown that setting people specific goals is more effective for generating work motivation and effort than setting general goals. In a review of the literature on this question, Locke, Shaw, Saari and Latham (1981) discuss 24 field experiments in all of which it was found that individuals given specific goals performed better than those only 'trying to do their best' or urged to surpass their own previous performance. Setting specific goals for people apparently concentrates their effort and attention on attempting to reach the specified goal. This work has been carried out principally in industrial psychology, but there are also studies in education demonstrating the advantageous effects of setting specific goals to school children (Anderson, 1985).

If we consider the Japanese school system in the light of this principle, it will be evident that the 'fourteen plus' entrance examinations for senior high schools and the entrance examinations for universities provide just such specific goals. Japanese school children aim to obtain entry to a specific senior high school or university. There are no comparable specific goals with such powerful motivational effects for the great majority of school children in Britain, the United States or Continental Europe. In the West the goals offered by teachers are more of the general 'try your best' type, which research in this area has found to be relatively ineffective.

(b) Effects of Proximate Sub-goals

It was recognised in the early theories of motivation formulated in the 1930s by Tolman (1932) and Lewin (1935) that people frequently order their goals in a causal chain so that they have to achieve a successive series of sub-goals in order to reach the ultimate goal. For example, a young person who wishes to become a doctor has to pass successive examinations (sub-goals) over a period of years before the final goal of full medical qualification and being able to work as a doctor is achieved. The young doctor may then envisage a further series of goals ahead consisting of rising in the medical profession. Much of human activity is structured in this way towards the achievement of successive sub-goals *en route* for more long term goals.

Research on the motivating effects of sub-goals has been reviewed by Bandura (1982). He describes a number of investigations on children where setting sub-goals has led to an improvement in performance. To explain this effect Bandura proposes that the presence of a sub-goal acts as an immediate incentive which mobilises motivation more powerfully than a distant incentive. Furthermore, the achievement of a sub-goal is a source of satisfaction and reinforcement for work effort. When one sub-goal has been achieved, the individual feels a sense of accomplishment or, in behaviourist terms, a reinforcement, and motivation to tackle the next sub-goal is enhanced.

Considered in the light of this principle, the examinations taken by school children can be usefully regarded as sub-goals on the way to securing desirable employment. The unique feature of the Japanese school system is that there exists such a powerful sub-goal for 14-year-olds in the form of the entrance examinations for the senior high schools. Virtually all Japanese children in the twelve to fourteen age group have to confront this sub-goal in the near future, and there is no comparable sub-goal for most children in this age range in Britain, the United States or Continental Europe.

(c) Motivating Properties of Challenging Goals

A number of studies first carried out by Locke (1968) and subsequently confirmed by others have shown that setting individuals challenging goals raises their motivation. A challenging goal is one which is difficult, but not impossible, for an individual to achieve. An easy goal is not challenging or motivating simply because it is too easy, while a very difficult goal is also not challenging because it is virtually impossible to attain. Most of the studies on which this conclusion is based have been conducted in field investigations in industry and in laboratory studies, but the general proposition has also been confirmed in studies of young children attempting discrimination between learning tasks of varying levels of difficulty (Masters, Furman and Barden, 1977). A review of 110 studies on this problem has concluded that 99 of them found that setting subjects challenging and specific goals produces better performances than easy, 'do your best', or no goals (Locke, Shaw, Saari and Latham, 1981). Setting individuals challenging goals appears to generate four effects which contribute to a high level of performance. Firstly, such goals direct attention to the task in hand; secondly, they increase the effort expended on the task; thirdly, they increase persistence and fourthly, they motivate individuals to develop improved strategies for solving the problem.

Once again the Japanese school system is so structured that it provides challenging goals and sub-goals for virtually all children. The hierarchically ranked senior high schools and universities have the effect that virtually all children can set their sights on a goal which is challenging for them. Clearly this is the case for able children attempting to pass the entrance examinations for the élite senior high schools and universities. But the system also provides challenging goals for those of moderate abilities who can set their sights on senior high schools and universities of good standing, although not the very best. Even children of less than average abilities have the incentives of attempting to secure entry to schools and colleges of some moderate standing, since admission to these is a good deal better than nothing, and is within the range of those with quite modest abilities. Thus the Japanese system is such that virtually all children are offered challenging goals and sub-goals in the form of attempting to secure entry, each according to his or her ability and effort, to high schools and universities of varying degrees of standing.

5.5 MARKS AND GRADES AS INCENTIVES

Up to this point in this chapter we have considered how effectively Japanese education operates as an incentive system. From this point onwards we consider the incentives for academic work provided for school children in the West, and note how these are in general weaker than those in Japan.

The principal incentives provided for school children in the West consist of the award of marks or grades for particular assignments. The child who does well is given an A or a B mark. These grades act as reinforcements for good work and serve as incentives for future work effort. This is well understood by teachers who award these marks in order to have this effect. It will probably come as no surprise to find that the widespread belief that grades and marks act as incentives for work effort has been sustained by a considerable number of research studies, which have been reviewed by O'Leary and Drabman (1971), Michaels (1977) and Slavin (1977).

There are, however, two weaknesses in the use of marks and grades as the most important incentives for academic work effort for school children in the West. In the first place they are not particularly powerful. Any individual mark is ephemeral and cumulatively they do not significantly affect a child's future career and social status. Secondly, it has often been pointed out that while marks and grades in Western schools act as incentives for children of high ability, they do not operate well for less able children. Children of high ability are capable of getting A or B grades and these, therefore, act as incentives. But children of lower ability are only capable of getting, C, D or E grades, and it is doubtful whether these function well as incentives for large numbers of less able children. This problem has been discussed by Michaels (1977) as it exists in typical American schools, and he concludes that the motivating and incentive effect of grades is largely confined to the top third of the ability range who are able with application to obtain A or B grades. The rest are simply discouraged. This problem of motivating children of moderate and low ability is not easy to overcome, but the Japanese school system is so structured that it goes a considerable way towards meeting it. It is difficult to avoid the conclusion that the reliance on the use of marks and grades as the principal incentives for academic work effort in Western schools is not as effective for large numbers of school children as the entrance examinations in Japan for hierarchically ranked senior high schools, which provide incentives for work effort for virtually all Japanese children.

5.6 THE INCENTIVE FUNCTION OF SELECTION FOR SECONDARY SCHOOLS IN BRITAIN, THE UNITED STATES AND CONTINENTAL EUROPE

In Britain and Continental Europe there were until relatively recently entrance examinations for élite secondary schools which bore some resemblance to those that still operate in Japan. It may therefore be thought that in Britain and Continental Europe the same motivating effects were achieved by these examinations, but a closer considera- tion of these systems will show that this was not the case. The selection system as it operated in Britain was typical of virtually the whole of Continental Europe. Secondary schools were of two kinds, namely prestigious academic grammar schools designed for intellectually able children, and unprestigious non-academic secondary modern schools designed for the intellectually less able. In Britain this dual system was established in 1944, although something resembling it went back to the late nineteenth century. Under the system set up in 1944, children took an examination at the ages of ten to eleven (the so-called 'eleven plus' examination) and on the basis of their performance were allocated to a grammar school or a secondary modern school. This system lasted until the 1960s and 1970s, when the system was largely phased out and the two kinds of schools amalgamated into comprehensive schools resembling American high schools. By the 1980s the grammar schools had almost entirely disappeared, although in most cities and towns of any size one or more independent grammar schools has remained, to which entry is secured on the basis of performance in entrance examinations set by the schools.

Similar systems prevailed in most of Continental Europe. The *lycées* in France, the *gymnasia* in West Germany and Sweden and similar academic schools in other countries of Continental Europe, closely resembled the British grammar schools. In most of Continental Europe the selection procedures for élite grammar schools were abolished in the 1960s and 1970s, as they have been in Britain, and the dual system has been replaced by comprehensive schools on the American model.

While these selection examinations prevailed in Britain and Continental Europe they undoubtedly provided an incentive for academic work for a number of children in the nine to eleven age range, as they approached the examinations. It was not uncommon for parents to purchase extra private coaching in the subjects tested in the examinations. An additional effect was that teachers were motivated to provide the instruction required for children in their charge to do well in the examinations. Superficially, therefore, the selection system which prevailed in Britain and most of Continental Europe appears to resemble the system operating in Japan. Nevertheless, while these selection procedures did provide incentives for children, they were not as effective as those in the Japanese system. The European procedures had two major disadvantages as compared with those in Japan. Firstly, only around 15 to 25 per cent of the child population, the precise proportion varying between countries and between localities within countries, passed these selection examinations and secured a place at an academic grammar school. Thus only around 25 to 35 per cent of 9 to 11-year-olds were ever serious candidates in the examination and exposed to its motivating and incentive effects. The remaining two-thirds or so of the children were unaffected by any incentive effects of the selection examinations.

Secondly, once the selection at the age of 11 years had been made the children were largely locked in to their respective types of school. Occasionally exceptionally able children who failed the entry examination obtained a transfer to a grammar school, but the great majority of the 75 to 85 per cent of children who failed to secure a place in a grammar school were labelled as failures and had no further goal or incentive for academic work. Most of these simply marked time in their second class schools until they reached the school leaving age, at which point they were permitted to leave and the great majority thankfully did so. There is no doubt that this was a dispiriting experience for the large majority of children who failed these examinations, and social surveys carried out in Britain while the system prevailed revealed a high level of demoralisation and dissatisfaction. Most children said they saw little point in being at school and hoped to leave as soon as possible (Morton-Williams and Finch, 1968).

The Japanese selection procedures for high schools avoid these two problems. Firstly, the ranking of all high schools in a finely graded status hierarchy, rather than the dichotomy of the European systems, has the effect of providing incentives for academic work for all children and not just a minority. Secondly, the crucial selection examinations in Japan are taken at the significantly later age of fourteen rather than at ten or eleven. Hence their incentive effects operate over the important years of early adolescence, during which the fate of the European child was already determined. In this way the demoralising effects for large numbers of adolescents of permanent consignment to inferior schools are avoided in the Japanese system. It will therefore be evident that although the European selection procedures for grammar schools bore some resemblance to the Japanese procedures, there are important differences which make the Japanese system far more effective for mobilising and sustaining work motivation for virtually all children throughout their years of compulsory education.

5.7 PUBLIC EXAMINATIONS AS INCENTIVES IN BRITAIN

In Britain an incentive function for school children to undertake academic work is provided by the public examinations of which the most important are the General Certificate of Education (GCE) 'O' Level and the Certificate of Secondary Education (CSE) taken normally at the age of sixteen, and the General Certificate of Education 'A' Level taken normally at the age of eighteen. Certificates are awarded on the basis of performance in these examinations and it is advantageous and frequently essential to obtain these certificates to secure employment or entry to universities and other institutions of tertiary education. It is important for British adolescents' future careers to pass these examinations and hence they serve as incentives for the academic work required. However, these incentive effects are confined to those who elect to take the examinations. The proportion of British teenagers taking these public examinations has gradually increased over the post-World War Two period. In the early post-war years only those at grammar schools took them, so that their motivating effects were confined to some 15 to 25 per cent of adolescents. Over the years the numbers taking these examinations have increased until by the mid-1980s the GCE or CSE examinations are taken by approximately 60 per cent of secondary school children.

In the early 1980s the British government, persuaded by academic analysis (Lynn, 1982b) of the important incentive effect of public examinations, introduced important reforms into the system. The GCE and CSE are to be replaced by a single examination to be known as the General Certificate of Secondary Education (GCSE), designed for the entire ability range. The significant feature of the new examination is that it will for the first time provide a goal for the less able 40 per cent of adolescents who have hitherto not been catered for. Perhaps the most remarkable aspect of this new school leaving certificate for all is that so many decades should have elapsed before it was realised by Ministers of Education and their advisers that less able adolescents are no different from the rest of mankind in needing goals to strive for if they are not to become demoralised.

5.8 MINIMUM COMPETENCE TESTS AS INCENTIVES IN THE UNITED STATES

Until relatively recently the United States has lacked the public certificated examinations which have for many years constituted an important incentive for academic work for more able adolescents in Britain. Historically, American adolescents obtained a high school graduation diploma so long as they remained in high school until late adolescence, irrespective of anything they might or might not have learned. The incentive for obtaining the graduation diploma was contingent on time spent in school, rather than on mastery of any academic curriculum, and hence had little if any effect on generating motivation for academic work.

In the 1970s some American educationists began to realise the deficiencies of this system. In several states they persuaded politicians to establish so-called minimum competence tests for the award of the high school graduation diploma. These were tests of basic elementary skills in reading and arithmetic and sometimes (varying in detail from state to state) in other academic subjects. The use of these minimum competence tests has spread rapidly in the United States and by the mid-1980s approximately three-quarters of the states had introduced them.

The objective of these tests has been to provide incentives for adolescents to acquire the basic skills of literacy and numeracy and to generate motivation to work for this end. There is a widespread measure of agreement in the United States that the minimum competence tests have had some success in achieving this objective. The weakness of the tests is that they only provide these incentives for the bottom 20 per cent or so of the ability range. The top 80 per cent or so acquire the basic skills of reading and arithmetic with the minimum expenditure of effort. Hence the tests provide no incentive for academic work effort for the great majority of American school children. Nevertheless, the establishment of minimum competence tests constitutes a recognition by American educationists of the weakness of the school system in the United States, from the point of view of the provision of incentives for academic work, and goes a small way towards rectifying this deficiency.

5.9 INCENTIVES FOR MASTERY OF AN ACADEMIC CURRICULUM

In many countries examinations for university entrance have an incentive function for adolescents in the 16- to 18-year-old age range to do the academic work required to secure entry to a university. Generally throughout Europe and in Japan there is a strong academic content in the curriculum tested in these examinations, and passes are only secured by those who have acquired a reasonably thorough knowledge of an academic discipline such as mathematics, physics, history and so forth. These examinations are either entrance examinations set by universities, as in Japan, or public examinations in which certain grades of pass are required, as in Britain. In Japan and Britain the more prestigious universities demand a high level of performance in these examinations, and all universities require an adequate performance from their prospective entrants. The effect of these examinations is to motivate adolescents aspiring to obtain entry to a university, and to as prestigious a university as possible, to master to the best of their abilities the academic curriculum tested in these examinations.

In the United States a different system is operated for university entrance. Entry to American universities is secured principally through performance in the Scholastic Aptitude Test (the SAT) or alternatively through the similar but less widely used American College Test (ACT). These tests are largely tests of aptitude, that is of ability and potential, rather than of academic knowledge, and their most important components are tests of verbal comprehension and of mathematical reasoning. The Scholastic Aptitude Tests are constructed by psychometricians at the Educational Testing Service in Princeton, and two of the test constructors (Messick and Jungeblut, 1981, p. 191) describe the test as follows:

> The SAT is not a measure of subject matter attainment such as the typical educational achievement test in biology or American history ... The SAT measures developed abilities of verbal and mathematical reasoning and comprehension that are acquired gradually over many years of experience and used in both school and non-school settings.

The effect of the use of the SAT for university entrance in the United States is that adolescents are not required to master an academic curriculum to the same degree that they are in Japan, Britain and much of Continental Europe. It is true that the SAT does also provide some achievement tests with academic content, and that one or two of these are taken by applicants to a small number of the most prestigious American universities. But even here these achievements tests play a relatively minor part in their selection procedure. Apart from these, it has been estimated by Harnett and Feldmesser (1980), on the basis of a sample survey of 200 four year American colleges, that four-fifths of American universities admit their students solely on the basis of the SAT aptitude tests, sometimes supplemented by school grades, and do not use any of the achievement tests. The effect of these university entrance procedures is that American adolescents are not required to acquire any profound knowledge of an academic discipline to secure entry to universities to anything like the extent that is required of adolescents in Japan, Britain or Continental Europe. There is little doubt that this is one of the major factors responsible for the relatively low academic standards of adolescents in the United States.

5.10 CO-OPERATION AND COMPETITION IN SCHOOLS

One of the advantages of external examinations in Japan and Britain is that they generate incentives for a class of children as a group. In this way they facilitate co-operation between children for the common objective of all performing well in these examinations, and at the same time they preserve the motivating effects of competition.

In the United States educationists have devoted much attention and research effort to the question of how competition and co-operation affect motivation and performance in general, and of school children in particular. The question is more complicated than may appear at first sight because there are a number of different competitive and co-operative situations. There is straightforward competition or co-operation between individuals; there are co-operating groups competing with other co-operating groups, as in the case of competing sports teams or commercial firms. There are also differences between tasks so that some tasks require co-operation among group members for their solution, as is normally the case for sports teams, and studies of these have naturally found that co-operation by group members produces better results than competition between group members. Useful reviews of the large number of studies in this area have been published by Michaels (1977) and Slavin (1977), both of whom conclude that competition between individuals is the most effective reward structure for enhancing academic performance.

This conclusion is readily understandable because in individual competitive situations the individual's success is directly contingent on his or her work effort, whereas in co-operative situations the success of the group is less dependent on the work effort of any individual group member and permits free-riders to enjoy the fruits of the work efforts of others.

In addition it has been shown by Johnson, Maruyama, Johnson, Nelson and Skon (1981) that co-operation between children for securing group goals can also be an effective condition for work effort, and in a later paper Johnson and Johnson (1983) propose that both competition and co-operation generate motivation and improve performance as compared with the absence of either of these conditions. These authors are sympathetic to attempting to foster co-operative behaviour in school children and they criticise American education on the grounds that American schools are too competitive and that 'despite the considerable amount of research indicating that co-operative learning has many advantages, current instruction in American is dominated by interpersonal competition and individualistic learning' (Johnson and Johnson, 1983, p. 120).

The reason for this emphasis by American teachers on competition is that this is the only effective motivator available to them. American teachers generate motivation through the award of grades. It is difficult to generate co-operative working groups in American schools because there are no external goals for the children to work for, such as the external examinations of Japan and, to a lesser extent, Europe. Hence the problem to which the two Johnsons have drawn attention.

The school system in Japan does not encounter this problem. Although the Japanese system is intensely competitive, far more so than in the United States, the competition is of a different kind. When Japanese children take their entrance examinations for their senior high schools and universities they are competing against thousands of other children in the locality or even, in the case of universities, in the country as a whole, but they are not competing against their classmates in the same classroom. On the contrary, in the Japanese classroom school children and their teachers are to a considerable degree engaged in a co-operative enterprise, working together to ensure that everyone does as well as possible. Several observers have noted this feature of Japanese schools. Vogel writes that 'the teacher becomes an ally who is trying to assist the student facing the examination' (Vogel, 1979, p. 165). The same function of generating co-operation within the classroom is served by the public examinations in Britain. It is the lack of external goals for school children in the United States which inevitably generates competition between individual children in the same classroom. The value of the external examinations as incentives for academic work is that they provide group goals towards which all children in a classroom can aspire without competing directly against one another.

5.11 CONCLUSIONS

In this chapter we have considered the incentives for academic work provided for school children in Japan, Britain, the United States and Continental Europe. Psychological research shows the importance of incentives in the generation of motivation for work effort of people in general, and school children in particular. In all countries teachers award marks and grades to fulfil an incentive function. There is no doubt that these do act as incentives for the more intellectually able children, but they are much less effective for the less able, who are only able to obtain moderate grades even with the exertion of considerable effort.

Public examinations also serve as incentives for academic work and are provided in a haphazard fashion in different countries for various categories of school children. In Britain the public examinations take at the age of sixteen act as an important incentive for the more intellectually able 60 per cent or so who taken them. The lower 40 per cent have no such incentives and are profoundly demoralised. The reverse of this situation is present in the United States, where the minimum competence tests in reading and arithmetic which have become generally required in recent years for the award of the high school graduation diploma act as incentives for the bottom 20 per cent or so of the ability range but not for the rest, who find them too easy. This contrasts between the public examinations in Britain and the United States, each making provision only for different sections of the ability range, is due to the failure of educationists in both countries to think through the importance of providing incentives for academic work for children of all abilities.

In virtually all countries older adolescents who aspire to a university are faced with significant incentives for academic work in the shape of the university entrance examinations. The exception here is the United States, where universities do not in general require anything like the detailed mastery of academic subjects from their prospective entrants that are demanded in Europe and Japan.

It is clear that the United States is the weakest of all the advanced nations so far as the provision of incentives for academic work for school children is concerned. The great majority of American children pass effortlessly from primary school to neighbourhood comprehensive. They are not confronted by the demanding public examinations taken by many British 16-year-olds, and they can secure entry to all but a handful of the most prestigious universities on the basis of their aptitudes as tested by the Scholastic Aptitude Test. At no point is the American school child actually required to learn anything. It is curious how little understanding has been shown by American educationists of this crucial weakness in American education.

While the European systems provide stronger incentives for school children for academic work that the United States, the European incentives are nowhere so powerful as those in Japan. There is little doubt that the different strengths of incentives for academic work are a major factor in the high educational standards achieved in Japan as compared with those of Europe and the United States.

6 The Intrinsic Motivation of Japanese School Children

In the last chapter the distinction was drawn between extrinsic and intrinsic motivation. It was argued that extrinsic motivation is exceptionally strong in Japanese school children because the external incentives which generate this form of motivation are themselves so powerful. In the present chapter we turn to intrinsic motivation, the motivation to work well in order to satisfy some internal value, standard or need.

The layman's term which most closely captures the concept of intrinsic motivation is *professionalism*. The individual whose work is characterised by professionalism is one who produces work of good quality, not for pecuniary gain, the fear of punishment or for other extrinsic reasons, but to satisfy an internal value that work ought to be done properly and to a high standard. This is undoubtedly an important source of motivation for the work of school children, as well as for that of adults, and many children work not merely for the marks they hope to receive or the examinations they hope to pass but also to satisfy these internal values. In this chapter we consider the nature of intrinsic work motivation, its origins and development, its strength in Japanese school children and its contribution to their high educational standards.

6.1 FOUR TYPES OF INTRINSIC WORK MOTIVATION

Psychologists and sociologists have distinguished four principal types of intrinsic work motivation and a description of these is given in the following section.

(a) The Protestant Work Ethic

Historically, the first conceptualisation of intrinsic motivation was advanced by Max Weber (1904), when he formulated the concept of the Protestant work ethic. Weber proposed that at the time of the

Reformation in sixteenth and seventeenth-century Europe, the Protestant sects developed a work ethic which was experienced as a moral duty to work hard and efficiently. He proposed further that this ethic was a crucial motivational factor, responsible for the economic and industrial achievement of the Protestant peoples of Northern Europe and North America in subsequent centuries. Weber's thesis has aroused controversy, but many scholars have concluded that it is plausible and it has received some substantiation by subsequent research (see, for example, Trevor-Roper, 1967).

Weber's Protestant work ethic has attracted the attention of psychologists. In recent years it has been shorn of its Protestant prefix because it has been found that it is no longer particularly strong in Protestants as compared with Roman Catholics or Jews. The strength of the work ethic in individuals has been measured by the construction of work ethic questionnaires, and it has been found by several investigators that the strength of the work ethic so measured is a determinant of work performance. For instance, we have found that the scores obtained on a work ethic scale by British school children make a significant contribution to their performance in the public examinations of GCE and CSE taken at the age of sixteen (Lynn, Hampson and Magee, 1983). Much of this work has been reviewed by Furnham (1984). The work ethic is therefore still regarded as an important form of intrinsic motivation and consists essentially of the belief that work should be done well as a moral duty.

(b) Achievement Motivation

A second form of intrinsic motivation which has been identified in contemporary psychology is achievement motivation. This concept has been formulated by McClelland and Atkinson and their colleagues (McClelland, 1961, 1985; Atkinson and Raynor, 1978; Dweck and Elliot, 1983). Achievement motivation is conceptualised as an internal motive to produce work of a high standard of excellence, and satisfaction is derived from the knowledge that the work has been done well. Although achievement motivation appears somewhat similar to the work ethic, the two types of motive are conceptually and empirically distinct. Achievement motivation lacks the explicitly moral component which is central to the work ethic. Some useful work on this distinction has been done by Spence and Helmreich (1983). They have constructed two separate questionnaire scales (labelled by them work and mastery) which are clearly identifiable as the work ethic and achievement motivation, and shown that the two traits are largely independent of each other and that both contribute to educational achievement among university students.

(c) Competitiveness

A third form of intrinsic motivation is competitiveness and consists of the motive to do better than others and achieve the symbols and substance of winning, such as achieving high status in hierarchical organisations, winning games and, in the case of school children, doing well in examinations. An early exponent of the importance of competitiveness as a motive was Alfred Adler, whose well-known concept of the inferiority complex consisted essentially of an acute awareness of inferiority which fuelled the competitive drive to secure improved status – 'By whatever name we give it, we shall always find in human beings this struggle to rise from an inferior position to a superior position, from defeat to victory, from below to above' (Adler, 1932). In contemporary psychology a questionnaire for the measurement of competitiveness has been constructed by Spence and Helmreich (1983). There has also been some treatment of competitiveness in personality theory where the concept appears as dominance (Cattell, 1979).

A number of sociobiologists have proposed that competitiveness has a genetic basis and is biologically programmed (for example, Wynne-Edwards, 1962; Wilson, 1975, 1978; Lopreato, 1984). This thesis rests on four propositions which are, to varying degrees, controversial. These are that competition for status, especially among males, is virtually universal in all human societies and throughout mammalian social species; that competitiveness emerges quite early in life and is clearly present among small boys by the ages of six and seven; that competitiveness secures survival advantages because those who are more competitive gain greater access to food and other resources as well as to mates; and that competitiveness as expressed in the personality trait of dominance has an appreciable genetic component in man (Cattell, Eber and Tatsuoka, 1970). Whether or not some genetic basis to competitiveness is regarded as plausible, there is little doubt that competitiveness is also developed in children to a greater or lesser extent by parents, teachers and other social influences.

(d) Competence Motivation

A fourth type of intrinsic motivation is termed competence motivation or effectance motivation. This is the motivation to explore, to learn, to understand the world and acquire mastery over it. It is evident from everyday observation that this form of motivation is strong in children and expresses itself in their curiosity, their enjoyment in solving puzzles and their desire to find out how things work and why things are as they are. It has been shown that this motivation to explore and learn about the environment is common in a large number of mammals, including rats and chimpanzees (Berlyne, 1950; Van Lawick-Goodall, 1967). A number of psychologists have considered that this motivation has a genetic and biologically programmed basis, since it clearly has survival value and is so common in mammals (for example, White, 1959; de Charms, 1968; Deci, 1975). Again, whether or not this is considered plausible, there is little doubt that this form of motivation is subject to development in children during the course of their upbringing.

6.2 THE DEVELOPMENT OF INTRINSIC MOTIVATION

It will be clear that intrinsic motivation has considerable importance for the efficient and productive performance of work. Both adults and school children will work better if they are activated by the intrinsic motives than if they are only motivated by external incentives. The importance of intrinsic motivation is such that a number of psychologists have been interested in the question of how this form of motivation comes to be acquired.

It may well be that some of the intrinsic motives, especially those of competitiveness and competence, are to some degree biologically programmed, as noted in the preceding section. Nevertheless, it is virtually universally accepted today that motives that are biologically programmed are subject to considerable modification in their strength and expression by environmental conditions experienced in childhood and adolescence (see, for example, Harter, 1981). The leading theory of the mechanism through which intrinsic motives are developed in children is that this takes place through conditioning processes involving the application of rewards and punishments administered principally by parents and teachers. The operation of these conditioning processes has been directly studied by McClelland and his associates, through investigations of the relationship between the achievement motivation levels of children and the style of child-rearing and socialisation adopted by their parents. This work has shown that it is parents who encourage independence and achievement who are responsible for children with high achievement motivation. The significance of the importance of parents' encouragement for independence is that children trained in that way come to feel personal responsibility for their own successes and failures (McCelland, 1961).

The conditioning processes through which parental rewards for independence and achievement are responsible for developing these as intrinsic motives in children lies in the Pavlovian mechanism of association. The child brought up in this way associates independence and achievement with approval, and comes in time to value these for their own sakes. Punishments may also play a part in this conditioning process, so that parental disapproval of their children's dependence, laziness or indifference in regard to their school achievement strengthens further the development of intrinsic motivations for personal responsibility and for work. An early formulation of this conditioning theory of socialisation was presented by Dollard and Miller (1950) and a recent formulation is given by Eysenck and Eysenck (1985)

An essentially similar conclusion in regard to the problem of how moral values come to be acquired as intrinsic motives has been reached by Kohlberg (1981). His extensive empirical work on this question has led to the view that in their early years children's motivations are solely determined by their anticipations of reward and punishment, which they have acquired from their past experiences. At this stage children's motivations are purely extrinsic. But gradually through the socialisation process these motivations become internalised and come to be felt as moral or quasi-moral values. Thus the young child who learns initially to tell the truth, be polite and so forth because of external rewards and punishments, comes in due course to regard these as morally right forms of behaviour. At this stage the motivation to behave in socialised ways has become intrinsic.

The motivation to work is one of many intrinsic motivations acquired in this way during the course of childhood and adolescence. The precise form in which this motivation is acquired, and whether it is felt as a moral obligation to work, conceptualised by Weber as the work ethic or in one of the other forms of achievement motivation, competitiveness or competence, is dependent on the style of upbringing by parents and the values that they themselves inculcate through their example and their methods of child-rearing. Whatever the variants of this form of motivation, they appear to be acquired through a long period of socialisation during which the child is exposed to the rewards and punishments which initially generate only extrinsic motivation.

6.3 INTRINSIC MOTIVATION IN JAPANESE CHILDREN

It was noted in Chapter 5 that Japanese children work considerably harder, do more homework, attend supplementary schools voluntarily and so on than those in the West. From this evidence alone it is not possible to determine whether Japanese children are activated by extrinsic motivation, that is simply the motivation to do well in forthcoming examinations, or by intrinsic motivation, the motivation to learn as an end in itself. No doubt both these motives are present in varying degrees in Japanese children, as in children elsewhere. There are, however, some studies which indicate that the level of intrinsic motivation for academic work is high among Japanese school children. The first evidence of this kind became available in the international study of achievement in mathematics carried out in the mid-1960s (Husen, 1967). Included in this survey was a questionnaire measuring attitudes to school work and consisting of such questions as 'I enjoy most of my school work and want to get as much additional education as possible'. This questionnaire provides a measure of the strength of intrinsic motivation for school work, since it is the essence of intrinsic motivation that work is enjoyed in itself and not undertaken in response to external incentives. In the mathematics study three samples of school children were investigated, namely 13-year-olds, 18-year-old mathematics specialists and 18-year-old non-mathematics specialists. Mean scores of these three samples from the twelve nations are shown in Table 6.1. It will be seen that the Japanese children score high on this attitude questionnaire. They obtain the highest score among the 13-year-olds and 18-year-old non-mathematicians, and are second to German children among the mathematicians. The correlation across countries for the 13-year-olds between these attitude scores and scores in the mathematics test is $+0.55$. National differences in the attitude scores from the 18-year-olds are less representative because of differential staying-on rates in different countries.

A similar questionnaire was used in the international survey of science achievement carried out in the early 1970s (Comber and Keeves, 1973). Here the age groups investigated were 10-year-olds and 14-year-olds. Again Japanese children scored high on the questionnaire although in this study they scored second to Hungary, which was not represented in the mathematics study. The scores from the different countries were calculated as standard scores on a mean of 0 and are shown in this form in Table 6.1. The correlations across countries between the strength of the favourable attitude to school work and science scores for the two science samples for 10- and 14-year-olds are + 0.21 and 0.45 respectively.

Table 6.1   Mean scores on attitude to school work questionnaires of 13- and 18-year-olds (mathematics study) and 10- and 14-year-olds (science study)

	13 yr olds M	*18 yr olds Ms*	*18yr olds N-m*	*10 yr olds Sc*	*14 yr olds Sc*
Australia	9.1	8.6	—	—	−09
Belgium	10.0	9.9	9.7	−02	05
England	9.3	8.5	8.5	05	07
Finland	—	10.5	10.5	−08	−16
France	10.4	9.7	9.6	—	—
Germany	—	10.7	10.5	−18	−26
Hungary	—	—	—	35	29
Israel	—	9.1	—	—	—
Italy	—	—	—	06	01
Japan	10.5	10.6	11.4	19	20
Netherlands	10.2	10.5	9.8	−19	−14
New Zealand	—	—	—	—	14
Scotland	9.1	8.7	8.5	05	03
Sweden	10.0	10.0	9.9	−36	−37
United States	8.4	8.0	8.3	14	19

Sources: Husen (1967); Comber and Keeves (1973)

There is further evidence for strong intrinsic motivation for academic work among Japanese children in the Minneapolis-Sendai study (Stevenson, 1983). As part of this investigation children were asked to express their attitude towards homework by selecting a smiling face, a neutral face or a frowning face. Among the 10-year-olds, 60 per cent of American children chose a frowning face as compared with slightly under 40 per cent of Japanese children. Thus although Japanese children do substantially more homework than American children, and might perhaps be considered by some Western educationists to be overburdened in this respect, they regard it more favourably than American children.

Finally, we consider a study of competitiveness in children in Japan, the United States, Belgium and Greece reported by Toda, Shinotsuka, McClintock and Stech (1978). The children in this study were boys and were 7-year-olds, 9-year-olds and 11-year-olds. The children played a game which was so constructed that they could display different degrees of competitiveness and hence a score for the strength of the children's competitiveness could be derived. The result showed that at all three age levels Japanese boys were far more competitive than those from the other three countries. There is little doubt that competitiveness – the drive to do better than others and to win – plays a part in the motivation of school children for academic work, and that therefore we have in this study further evidence for the strength of this motivation among Japanese children. It is interesting to note that Japanese children are more competitive than those elsewhere by the early age of seven, showing that this motivation is well established at this relatively early age.

6.4 THE ROLE OF PARENTS IN THE ACQUISITION OF INTRINSIC MOTIVATION

Parents are the primary agents in the socialising of children, and the strong intrinsic motivation of school children must be attributed to a considerable extent to the socialisation procedure adopted by Japanese parents. The processes that take place can be envisaged as follows. Japanese parents are well aware of the importance for their children of obtaining the educational credentials of graduation from a high status senior high school and university, and they transmit their concern for educational achievement to their children during the course of their upbringing. A close observer of Japanese society writes that 'the anxieties of Japanese parents for the cognitive achievement of their children easily outdistances that of American parents', and in corroboration of this notes that attitude surveys in Japan show that when Japanese men are asked to rate the qualities they look for in a wife they give devotion to the children's education a very high ranking (Cummings, 1980, pp. 80, 115).

The concern of Japanese parents for educational achievement is expressed in the very high proportion, approximately 70 per cent, who are willing to pay fees for kindergarten to give their children an early start. During the middle years of childhood large numbers of Japanese parents are willing to spend further sums on giving their children extra coaching at the *juku* and on sending them to the fee paying senior high schools and universities. The financial sacrifices which Japanese parents make to provide their children with a good education are far greater than those in the West and are testimony to the concern felt on this matter by Japanese parents.

There is in addition direct evidence for the role played by Japanese parents in socialising their children for achievement, collected by Tanner (1977). In this study a comparison was made between the child-rearing practices and values of 100 Japanese parents of kindergarten children in the city of Okinawa, and those of a matched sample of American parents. The author draws attention to the way in which many Japanese mothers devote much effort to developing their children's language skills and to teaching them to read and do simple arithmetic, and that the Japanese mothers are more concerned with this early cognitive socialisation than American mothers.

Furthermore, when the parents were asked to rank eight of their children's developmental processes in order of importance, Japanese parents ranked *self-help* first, while American parents ranked *emotional adjustment* first and *self-help* fourth. Training children for self-help is essentially the same as the independence training investigated by McClelland (1961) and his associates, and it will be recalled that McClelland's group have found that it is precisely parents who stress independence training in their socialisation practices who produce children with high achievement motivation. Tanner's study therefore provides direct evidence that Japanese parents tend to use the appropriate socialisation techniques for developing strong intrinsic work motivation in their children, namely independence training and the early encouragement of academic skills.

The most extensive investigation comparing the concern of Japanese and American parents for their children's educational achievement is the Minneapolis-Sendai study carried out by Stevenson (1983) and his colleagues. They collected measures both of parents' behaviour indicative of the encouragement of educational achievement and also of parents' attitudes. So far as behaviour is concerned, the investigations noted the extent to which parents in Japan and the United States had bought their children educational books and desks to work at. They found that 98 per cent of Japanese 10-year-olds had their own desk at home as compared with 63 per cent of American 10-year-olds. Among Japanese parents, 58 per cent had bought their children mathematics work books for extra study and 29 per cent science work books. Among American parents, those who had made these purchases were 28 per cent and 1 per cent respectively.

A comparison between Japan and the United States of the degree to which parents give help to their children with their homework tells the same story. According to the mothers' own reports, Japanese mothers helped their children with homework for an average of 24 minutes a day for 6-year-olds and 19 minutes a day for 10-year-olds; in the case of American mothers these figures were 14 and 15 minutes a day. The Taiwanese mothers also investigated in this study behaved like the Japanese mothers both as regards help with homework and the purchase of desks and school books.

Similar differences between Japanese and American mothers were found when attitudes towards schools and educational achievement were studied by means of questionnaires. Three areas of beliefs were investigated. Firstly, mothers were asked how they rated their child's general educational standard, achievement in mathematics and intellectual ability. Secondly, how they rated the school and how good a job it was doing; and thirdly, how they rated the relative importance of effort and ability in the educational standards achieved by children. The results of this study are set out in Table 6.2.

Table 6.2   Comparison of mothers' attitudes to children's abilities and the effectiveness of schools in Japan, the United States and Taiwan

Mothers' ratings	Japan	United States	Taiwan
Child's Ability	5.5	6.3	6.1
Child's Maths Achievement	5.8	5.9	5.2
Academic performance v. satisfactory	5%	42%	5%
Schools doing good job	39%	91%	42%
Importance of effort	5.2	3.9	4.4
Importance of ability	2.3	3.3	2.7

Source: Stevenson *et al.* (1983)

The mothers' evaluations of their children's abilities are given in the first three rows of Table 6.2. These evaluations were made on a 9 point scale running from 'much below average' = 0 to 'average' = 5 to 'much above average' = 9. Looking first at the mothers' ratings of their children's abilities, it will be seen that American mothers were more satisfied in this regard than Japanese mothers (6.3 as against 5.5), although mothers in all three countries consider that their own children have above average ability. Perhaps mothers everywhere have this unrealistically favourable view of the native intellectual endowments of their offspring! There were virtually no differences between Japanese and American mothers in their views of their children's standards of achievement in mathematics, although considered objectively the standards are considerably higher in Japan.

It is the data in the third row that show the most striking national differences. Here 42 per cent of American mothers consider that their children's academic performance is 'very satisfactory' as against only 5 per cent in Japan. Similar differences were also found in mothers' evaluations of whether the schools were doing a good educational job. In the United States 91 per cent of mothers considered that the schools attended by their children were doing a good job, but only 39 per cent of Japanese mothers gave this favourable rating to the schools. It appears, therefore, that Japanese mothers have higher expectations of schools and are less satisfied with them than American mothers.

The final two rows of Table 6.2 give the mothers' estimates of the importance of effort and ability as determinants of children's educational achievement. Japanese mothers tend to stress effort (5.2 as against 3.9), whereas American mothers tend to stress ability (3.3 as against 2.3). It seems that these differences reflect a greater belief in the importance of work effort as the major determinant of educational achievement among Japanese mothers. The attitudes of American mothers are more fatalistic, attaching relatively less significance to work effort and more significance to ability. All these results suggest that Japanese mothers are likely to exert more psychological pressure for achievement on their children than American mothers.

6.5 COMPLEMENTARY RELATIONSHIP BETWEEN EXTRINSIC AND INTRINSIC MOTIVATION

It has been argued that the strong external incentives for educational achievement in Japanese society act on parents as well as directly on children. Japanese parents respond to these incentives and transmit their concern for achievement to their young children through the normal conditioning and socialisation processes. Japanese children initially develop extrinsic motivation for academic work, but during the course of childhood this becomes internalised as intrinsic motivation. By the time they are adolescents intrinsic motivation is an important component in the total academic motivation of Japanese teenagers, although the external incentives remain strong and sustain extrinsic motivation as well. According to this view strong extrinsic motivation is the basis on which strong intrinsic motivation subsequently develops.

This view is different from that held by a number of educationists who have regarded extrinsic and intrinsic motivations as independent, or even mutually incompatible, forms of motivation. Those who hold this view normally consider that intrinsic motivation for academic work is desirable and extrinsic motivation is objectionable, and therefore that the incentives that generate extrinsic motivation (marks, grades, examinations and so forth) should be minimised or entirely abolished. The teacher's objective should be to develop only children's intrinsic motivation, the pursuit of learning for its own sake and not merely to gain marks, competitive success, status and social approval. Statements by prominent educationists of this commonly-held position will be found in Peters (1965) and Kelly (1980).

The view presented in this chapter is different. It is common ground that intrinsic motivation – the pursuit of learning for its own sake and enjoyed as an end in itself – is valuable and efforts should be made to foster this form of motivation in school children. However, the argument here is that intrinsic motivation develops as a consequence of the external incentive system which initially only generates extrinsic motivation to secure marks, grades and parental and social approval. The leading psychological theories of socialisation as formulated by Dollard and Miller (1950), McClelland (1961), Kohlberg (1981) and Eysenck and Eysenck (1985) all hold that intrinsic motivation is built up on the basis of extrinsic motivation. This view has a strong appeal to common sense. Consider the child's acquisition of the value of cleanliness. It is a matter of everyday observation that young children have little intrinsic motivation to wash and keep themselves clean. The young children who beg to be allowed to wash their hands before meals are few indeed. Initially, young children have to be cajoled into washing. But after years of the pressures of socialisation, children gradually come to acquire intrinsic motivation for cleanliness and at this stage they wash voluntarily because they would rather be clean than dirty. The leading theorists of socialisation maintain that many and perhaps all intrinsic motivations are acquired in this way, including work motivation. The strong work motivation of Japanese school children appears to be a special case of these general principles. The pressures and incentives for academic work for Japanese school children are exceptionally powerful, and these initially generate strong extrinsic motivation for work. This strong extrinsic motivation comes in time to generate strong intrinsic motivation, and in the later school years Japanese adolescents enjoy learning more than their counterparts in the West (see Table 6.1, where the evidence for this is set out). The Japanese experience, therefore, confirms the leading models of the socialisation process in suggesting that the way to promote children's intrinsic motivation for academic work is through a system of strong incentives such as marks, grades and examinations. These will initially generate strong extrinsic motivation for academic work and on the basis of this intrinsic motivation will develop. The relationship between intrinsic and extrinsic motivation is not the incompatibility suggested by a number of educationists, but is one of complementarity.

6.6 CONCLUSIONS

Intrinsic work motivation consists of motivation to satisfy some internal standard or value, rather than to secure an external incentive. Four principal variations of intrinsic motivation can be distinguished, namely the work ethic, achievement motivation, competitiveness and competence motivation. It may be that some of these have a genetic basis. Whether or not this is the case, they are certainly developed during the course of childhood through parental socialisation in stressing independence and achievement.

These socialisation techniques are employed by Japanese parents and are largely responsible for the transmission of strong intrinsic work motivation from parents to children and for the high level of this motivation in Japanese school children. A number of educationists in the West see an incompatibility between intrinsic and extrinsic motivation. They have argued that extrinsic motivation generated through the use of marks, examinations and so forth should be minimised in order to promote intrinsic motivation, the pursuit of learning for its own sake. Leading contemporary theories of socialisation suggest that this view is incorrect. On the contrary, it is through a strong system of incentives for work effort that children who initially work from extrinsic motivation come to develop intrinsic motivation. The Japanese experience strengthens this view. Young Japanese children have stronger extrinsic work motivation than those in the West because the incentives for work are more powerful. But by the time they are adolescents Japanese school children have acquired stronger intrinsic work motivation. At this stage they work harder than children in the West because they actually enjoy their school work more.

7 The Contribution of Teachers and Schools to Educational Achievement

The educational achievements of children are a product not only of the characteristics of the children themselves, but also of their teachers and their schools. It is to the significance of this input into educational achievement in Japan that we now turn. Few will doubt that an important contribution to children's educational achievement lies in their teachers' professionalism, their dedication to learning, their enthusiasm, professional skills and conscientiousness in the thorough preparation of lessons and marking of homework. A review by Parkerson, Schiller, Lomax and Walberg (1984) of 95 studies carried out in the United States gives a mean correlation of $+0.81$ between the quality of teachers' instruction and the educational achievement of their children.

In this chapter we start by reviewing evidence for the high level of professionalism of Japanese teachers. We consider next the factors responsible for this high level of professionalism, including the specification of the curriculum by government, the competition between high schools and the role of private schools; considered next are teachers' abilities, training and remuneration; the financial resources available to schools and the teacher/pupil ratio and, finally, the amount of time devoted to school work.

7.1 THE PROFESSIONALISM OF JAPANESE TEACHERS

Western observers of Japanese schools have testified to the high levels of professionalism of Japanese teachers. An American anthropologist, Thomas Rohlen, spent a year observing Japanese high schools in Kobe and observed that Japanese teachers would quite frequently telephone parents in the evenings to discuss their children's progress or, alternatively, they would call at parents' houses, and that this degree of commitment would be unheard of in the United States (Rohlen, 1983). The effectiveness of the discipline maintained by Japanese teachers has frequently been noted.

In a study comparing Japanese and American teachers in this regard made by Cummings (1980) in the 1970s, the author was impressed by the professionalism of Japanese teachers in maintaining order, and noted how this was established in classes for 6-year-olds from the very start of their school experiences. He estimated that the typical Japanese teacher spent 10 to 20 per cent of the time keeping order, while in the United States around 40 per cent of time was devoted to this objective. He describes the air of purposeful learning in the Japanese classroom, compared with which the American classroom is, in the author's own words, more like a carnival. While this is no doubt partly due to the superior socialisation of Japanese children, the professionalism of Japanese teachers must also make a contribution to the good order typically found in Japanese classrooms.

It is not easy to obtain objective measures of the professionalism of teachers, since what goes on in the classroom is difficult to quantify or even observe. Perhaps the best approach to this problem is to take the evaluations of teachers made by their own pupils. The first investigation to collect comparative data of this kind was the international study of achievement in mathematics (Husen, 1967). As part of this investigation pupils in twelve economically advanced nations answered a questionnaire on their teachers' methods of instruction. This consisted of such questions as 'My mathematics teacher shows us different ways of solving the same problem' and 'My mathematics teacher requires the pupils not only to master the steps in solving problems, but also to understand the reasoning involved'. It appears that this is essentially a measure of the teachers' professionalism as evaluated by pupils, the more highly professional teacher being those who explain different ways of solving problems and the reasoning involved in the solutions. The results showed that among 13-year-olds Japanese children awarded their teachers the highest scores on this questionnaire. Among the 18-year-olds mathematics specialists Japanese adolescents also awarded their teachers a high score, this time fractionally second to those in Israel. The correlations between pupils' perceptions of teachers' professionalism and mathematics achievement across countries are 0.86 (P<.01) for the 13-year-olds and 0.25 for the 18-year-olds.

A second source of data on Japanese teachers' professionalism comes from the comparison of schools in Minneapolis and Sendai, made by Stigler, Lee, Lucker and Stevenson (1982). One finding in this investigation concerns the amount of homework done by children in Japan and the United States. It was found that 6-year-olds in Sendai spent 233 minutes per week on homework as compared with 79 minutes in Minneapolis. Among 10-year-olds Japanese children did 368 minutes of homework per week compared with 256 minutes by American children.

Part of the reason for these national differences is that Japanese teachers consider homework more important than American teachers. Asked to rate the importance of homework on a 9 point scale (9 = very important, 1 = unimportant), Japanese teachers gave a mean rating of 5.8 and American teachers 4.4 (Taiwanese teachers gave 7.3) (Stevenson, 1983). Hence Japanese teachers believe more strongly in the importance of homework, set more homework and ensure that it is done. It seems reasonable to infer that this reflects a greater professional commitment to efficient education on the part of Japanese teachers.

In a further part of this study reported by Stevenson *et al.* (1985), detailed observations were made of the classroom behaviour of both children (6-year-olds and 10-year-olds) and teachers in 40 classrooms. The gist of the conclusions was that classrooms in Japan are far more disciplined than in the United States. Japanese children spend more time sitting quietly and listening to their teacher, while American children spend more time working or purportedly working on individual assignments, in small groups, or in non-work activities, such as wandering around the classroom or chatting to other children. The overall finding was that the Japanese children spent 66 per cent of their time attending to instruction as compared with only 46 per cent in the case of American children.

It would appear that what has been captured in these observations is a difference in professionalism between Japanese and American teachers. The authors of the report do not put it exactly like this, but they do conclude that 'Americans appear to expect elementary school children to accomplish much more on their own than they are capable of'. This appears to be a tactful way of saying that American teachers consider it less their own responsibility to teach children and more the responsibility of children to learn for themselves, or that there is a relative abnegation of the responsibility to teach on the part of American teachers.

7.2 GOVERNMENT SPECIFICATION OF THE CURRICULUM

In considering the question of why Japanese teachers should display such a high degree of professionalism and commitment it is proposed that the first important factor is detailed specification of the curriculum by government. The Japanese Ministry of Education sets out in detail the curriculum which has to be taught in schools. Some degree of government specification of the curriculum is also present in most of the countries of continental Europe, including France, West Germany, Holland and Belgium, but these countries do not have the detailed specifications set out in Japan. Britain and the United States are unusual among economically advanced nations in the freedom of schools from the requirement to follow curricula laid down by government. In Britain the curriculum is under the control of head teachers and the government has no power to direct what should be taught. A broadly similar degree of autonomy generally prevails in the United States, where the content of the curriculum is normally determined by head teachers in conjunction with local education officials.

It is inevitable that the autonomy of head teachers in the determination of the curriculum in Britain and the United States will entail considerable variation between schools in what is actually taught, and that because of this variation there will be many schools where subjects will be taught less thoroughly than in a country like Japan, where the curriculum is specified in detail by government. A critical look at education in the United States from this point of view has been taken by the American educationist David Berliner. He reviews evidence from studies which have shown a great range in the amount of time teachers in different schools devote to the basic subjects. For instance, in a study of primary schools it was found that some teachers devoted 40 to 50 minutes a day to teaching reading, while others devoted almost three times as much time to this fundamental skill. In arithmetic some teachers entirely omitted to teach fractions, while others teaching children of the same age covered fractions very thoroughly and devoted 32 hours a year to them. It appears that although the curriculum is normally determined in American schools by head teachers and local education officials, in practice teachers are monitored and evaluated very little. Even the head teachers have only a very vague idea of what is actually being taught in individual classrooms. Berliner concludes that American teachers have no clear sense of purpose and that, in his own words, 'what is seen in classrooms more often resembles baby-sitting than it does education' (Berliner, 1985, p. 128).

There is clear evidence that the decentralised control of the curriculum in Britain and the United States has led to basic subjects being less thoroughly taught than in Japan. In both the first

Table 71   Teachers' estimates of coverage of the curriculum for 13-year-olds
in maths and 14-year-olds in science

	Maths	*Science*		*Maths*	*Science*
Australia	–	203	Italy	–	186
Belgium	–	193	Japan	63.1	296
England	60.4	179	Netherlands	–	137
Finland	47.4	151	New Zealand	–	215
France	49.9	–	Scotland	51.3	190
Germany FR	–	182	Sweden	37.4	188
Hungary	–	278	United States	47.5	198
Israel	65.7	–			

Sources: Husen (1967); Comber and Keeves (1973)

international study of mathematics and of science (Husen, 1967;
Comber and Keeves, 1973) the syllabus which 13- and 14-year-olds
ought to have was drawn up by an international panel of educationists,
and on the basis of this the tests used in the two investigations were
constructed and administered to representative schools in a number of
countries. As part of the investigations, the teachers were asked to
judge how far the material in the tests had been taught in their own
schools. The results of these teacher judgments are shown in Table
7.1. It will be seen that the coverage of the syllabus was very thorough
in Japan, where the highest index number for coverage was given for
science and the second highest for mathematics. The correlations
between the thoroughness of the coverage of the curriculum and the
mean scores obtained on the tests were 0.64 and 0.80 for mathematics
and science respectively. Both of these correlations are statistically
significant and indicate that across nations an important determinant
of educational achievement is the extent to which the syllabus tested
has been taught. There can be little doubt that an important reason for
the thorough coverage of the syllabus in Japanese schools lies in the
fact that the curriculum is specified by government.

   Further evidence on this question came to light in the detailed
comparison of the curriculum taught in mathematics in Japanese and
American primary schools which was made by Stigler, Lee, Lucker
and Stevenson (1982) in their Minneapolis-Sendai study. They found
that Japanese schools introduce a number of mathematical concepts
and skills earlier than American schools and argue persuasively that
this is one of the reasons that Japanese children are ahead of American

children in mathematical attainment. The reason that Japanese teachers introduce these mathematics skills earlier is that they are required to do so.

It is difficult to escape the conclusion that the presence of a curriculum stipulated by government and monitored by schools' inspectors imposes a discipline on teachers which is lacking in Britain and the United States. Without these government guidelines there is bound to be a certain lack of direction and sense of purpose in British and American schools. It seems certain that a control system of the kind operated in Japan must play a significant role in maintaining the efficiency of teachers.

7.3 COMPETITION BETWEEN SCHOOLS

It is considered that the second important factor for the efficiency of Japanese teachers lies in the degree of competition between schools. Japanese high schools compete for examination successes and for good pupils who are likely to achieve these successes. To some degree this competition is present between the junior high schools, but it is considerably stronger among the senior high schools. An important element in this competition between high schools is the large amount of publicity given by the media to schools' examination results and the ranking of schools in public esteem on this basis. The effect of this is that teachers' self-esteem becomes bound up with their schools' examination successes. This provides a powerful incentive for Japanese teachers to work efficiently in order to maintain the public reputation of their schools.

The invigorating effects of competition on Japanese teachers' efficiency can be regarded as a special case of the more general principle that competition tends to increase people's work effort. This proposition is widely accepted in both economics and psychology. In economics this principle commands such general assent that governments in all advanced western nations have agencies to ensure that competition is maintained among commercial firms and that these do not collude to avoid competition through the establishment of monopolies or cartels. In sectors of the economy where competition does not exist, as for instance among state schools in Britain and the United States, a number of economists have attempted to devise methods by which competition could be introduced in order to achieve an increase in efficiency. A review of such proposals for breaking up the monopoly of state schools has recently been published by Seldon (1986).

The stimulating effects of competition have also been recognised in psychology. Competition operates both between individuals and between groups and at both levels it enhances work effort (see, for example, Michaels (1977), and Slavin (1977) for reviews of the literature on the work-enhancing effects of competition among school children). So far as Japanese teachers are concerned, the stimulating effects of competition are largely a group phenomenon, because schools compete with one another as units and it is through the successes of the school as a whole, rather than through those of the individual teacher, that teachers derive their standing in the community.

The psychological motives that are generated among the members of groups which find themselves in competition are two-fold. The first is competitiveness and the second is the maintenance of self-esteem. In regard to competitiveness, it is a matter of everyday observation that humans readily identify with the groups to which they belong and will strive to secure the success of their own group over competing groups. This propensity manifests itself quite early in life when children will identify with their school, football team and so forth and work for their group's competitive success, apparently for the satisfaction of seeing their group winning. There is no doubt that adults are equally powerfully motivated to work for the competitive success of the groups with which they identify, such as their political party, their firm and their nation in time of conflict and war. The classical psychological studies of group identification and competitiveness were carried out by Sherif and Sherif (1953) in their studies of boys at a summer camp in the United States. The boys were divided into two groups and it was shown that group identification, competitiveness, conflict and hostility between these two groups were extraordinarily easily mobilised.

Two principal theories have been advanced to explain this human disposition of people to work for the competitive success of the groups to which they belong. The first is social learning theory, which attributes this propensity to training and socialisation by parents and schools during childhood and adolescence. The classical work is that of Margaret Mead, the social anthropologist who described the lifestyles of a number of different tribes in South East Asia in the 1930s. Some of these tribes were highly competitive and others less so, and differences were attributed to differences in socialisation and social learning during childhood (Mead, 1935). The second theory has been advanced by sociobiologists and posits a biologically programmed disposition for group competitiveness. This theory proposes that among social species, including man, groups or tribes that competed successfully against other groups increased their chances of survival and reproduction. The more successful groups were able to enlarge their territory and grow in numbers. For this reason there has evolved genetic programming for group identification and competitive striving against any rival group with which a group finds itself in competition for resources. This theory has a long pedigree. It was first put forward by Darwin in his later book *The Descent of Man* (Darwin, 1871) and was elaborated by Spencer (1892) and Keith (1948). In recent times the leading exponents of this thesis are Durham (1976) and Wilson (1978).

In addition to competitiveness, a second motive which is mobilised in conditions of competition is that of self-esteem. The significance of this motive has been analysed by Zander (1971, 1980). He proposes that an important determinant of people's self-esteem lies in the standing of the groups to which they belong. People experience pride when their group achieves successes and humiliation when their group suffers reversals, in the same way that as individuals they experience pride or humiliation in their own personal successes and reversals. It is therefore proposed that the motivation of groups obeys the same laws as that of individuals. Group successes act as rewards because they enhance pride in the group's achievements, while group reversals act as punishments because they generate feelings of humiliation. Groups placed in a competitive environment experience a challenge to their self-esteem. They can anticipate the psychologically rewarding benefits of group achievements and the painful consequences of failures, and will expend work effort to achieve successes for their group and to avoid reversals. This formulation is supported by a number of empirical studies showing that people will work harder if they are told that their work effort will contribute to the success of their group than if they are told that they are only working for themselves.

It is easy to see how the competition that exists between Japanese high schools is likely to generate these motives of competitiveness and the maintenance of self-esteem among Japanese teachers. The public standing of the Japanese teachers is to a considerable extent determined by the reputation of their schools, and this is itself determined by the schools' examination successes. These sources of motivation are very much weaker in the West, where schools do not compete for the esteem of the public to anything like the extent that they do in Japan.

7.4 PRIVATE SCHOOLS

It is proposed that the third factor contributing to the efficiency of Japanese teachers lies in the strength of the private sector in Japanese education. This operates in two principal ways. Firstly, there are the entirely commercial private coaching establishments (the *juku*), which provide supplementary education in the evenings, at weekends and in the school holidays. It is not possible to disentangle the contribution of the *juku* from that of the normal schools to the education standards achieved by Japanese children, but as approximately half of Japanese children attend these supplementary education establishments their contribution must be considerable. Secondly, among senior high schools there are large numbers of private schools amounting to approximately 30 per cent nationally and 40 to 50 per cent in the large cities.

The contribution of the large private sector in Japanese education can be understood in terms of the general theorem of economics that goods and services provided by private competing institutions (generally firms) are produced more efficiently than those provided by either public competing institutions or public monopolies. The explanation normally advanced by economists for the superior efficiency of private competing suppliers is that they are subjected to what is termed 'the discipline of the market'. Economists do not spell out the psychological nature of this discipline, but what is meant is apparently that competing private suppliers are motivated by fear. Such suppliers are conscious that if they do not produce their services efficiently they will lose their customers and their firm will go bankrupt. It is this threat of bankruptcy that makes the motivation of private suppliers stronger than that of public suppliers. It is possible for public suppliers to operate in competition, but when this is the case the fear that inefficiency will entail bankruptcy is either absent or considerably weaker than in the case with private suppliers. For instance, British universities are public institutions that compete for good students for financial resources, but those who work in British universities are not motivated by fear that if they do poorly in this competition they will be faced with bankruptcy and unemployment. Fear is a strong motive and there is little doubt that its presence is an important factor in the generally superior efficiency of private competing institutions.

In the case of the Japanese senior high schools the large number of private schools has three effects that deserve comment. Firstly, these private high schools are themselves kept efficient by their direct accountability to parents. The teachers in them are conscious that if they cease to be efficient parents would remove their children and the schools would be forced to close. Secondly, while only some 40 to 50 per cent of the senior high schools in Japanese cities are private institutions, their existence exerts some pressure for efficiency on the public schools. If standards in the public schools started to fall significantly below those in the private schools, there would be a public outcry and a demand for improvement. The private schools serve as a yardstick of efficiency against which the public schools are judged.

A third feature of the Japanese senior high schools is that the permissible school leaving age in Japan is set quite low, namely at the age of fifteen as compared with sixteen in Britain (Approximately sixteen and a half in practice) and sixteen to seventeen in different states of the United States. The voluntary nature of education at the Japanese senior high schools exerts further pressure on these schools to be efficient, since Japanese teenagers can quit education altogether if they do not like what they find there. The compulsory nature of education for much of this age group in Britain and the United States provides teachers with a captive market and is a further factor leading to reduced efficiency.

7.5 TEACHERS' ABILITIES

Ability is widely believed to be an important determinant of the efficiency with which jobs are performed. Professions, commercial firms and employers generally endeavour to select employees who have good ability and frequently use examination certificates as a measure of this. Considerable evidence for an association between ability and productivity has been collected by Schmidt and Hunter (1981), who conclude that ability is a valid predictor of the efficiency of performance in a wide range of jobs.

The question therefore needs to be asked of whether Japanese schools tend to recruit teachers of greater ability than those elsewhere and if this is a factor in their professionalism and competence. Comparative evidence for a number of economically advanced nations has been collected by Passow, Noah, Eckstein and Mallea (1976). They categorised entrants to the teaching profession in different countries according to whether they were typically above average as compared with college and university students as a whole, average, or below average. These comparisons were made for both primary and secondary school teachers and the results are set out in Table 7.2.

Table 7.2   Abilities of teachers at primary and secondary schools

Primary Schools	Secondary Schools
1. *Above average* Japan Sweden	1. *Above average* Netherlands Scotland
2. *Average* Belgium England Germany Hungary Netherlands Scotland	2. *Average* Belgium Hungary Japan N. Zealand
3. *Below average* Italy	3. *Below average* Italy

Source: Passow *et al.* (1976)

These data are not adequate for statistical treatment. Impressionistically, it can be observed that at the primary school stage both Japan and Sweden attract teachers of high ability and 10-year-olds in both these countries did well in the international study of achievement in science (see Table 2.3 in Chapter 2). On the other hand, Italian children with apparently weak teachers do no worse than children in the six countries with teachers of average abilities. At the secondary school stage there appears to be no relation at all between the abilities of teachers and the educational achievements of children. Japan and Hungary are the two countries which consistently do well in all the international surveys reviewed in Chapter 2, yet they only recruit teachers of average abilities. Conversely, The Netherlands and Scotland attract the most able recruits into the teaching profession, but the children from these two countries do not do particularly well in the international studies of achievement. Taking the pattern of results as a whole, it may be that the recruitment of teachers of high ability makes a contribution to Japanese educational standards at primary school level, but this is not the case among secondary schools.

7.6 TEACHERS' TRAINING AND QUALIFICATIONS

A further characteristic of teachers that deserves consideration is their training and qualifications. It is widely believed that teachers should be well educated and highly trained, and in all economically advanced nations the length of training of teachers has been increased over the course of this century in the expectation that as a result they will be more effective in the classroom. International data on this question were collected by Comber and Keeves (1973) for fourteen developed nations. These are shown in Table 7.3 as the number of years spent in tertiary education by primary and secondary school teachers. It will be

Table 7.3   Length of tertiary education of primary and secondary school teachers

Country	Primary	Secondary	Country	Primary	Secondary
Australia	–	3.7	Italy	1.1	4.2
Belgium	1.7	2.8	Japan	2.7	3.7
England	2.3	3.3	Netherlands	3.3	2.8
Finland	3.2	4.4	N. Zealand	–	3.8
France	–	2.0	Scotland	3.2	4.3
Germany	3.6	4.1	Sweden	2.1	3.7
Hungary	0.9	3.7	USA	4.5	4.8

Source: Comber and Keeves (1973)

seen that, considered in this international context, both primary and secondary school teachers in Japan have about the average amount of training. The lengthiest training of teachers occurs in the United States, where the educational standards achieved tend to be low. The correlations between the length of training of teachers and children's achievements in the first international mathematics study and the science study have been calculated. The correlation between the length of training of primary school teachers and the achievement of 10-year-olds in science is zero. The correlations between the length of training of secondary school teachers and the achievement of

13-year-olds in mathematics is -0.26, and of 14-year-olds in science $+0.22$. Neither of these correlations are statistically significant. It seems, therefore, that the amount of education and training received by teachers in different countries is not a significant determinant of the educational standards achieved by children.

7.7 TEACHERS' REMUNERATION

A further factor which is frequently believed to determine the efficiency with which work is performed is remuneration. High pay, it is commonly argued, attracts a good quality of recruit, provides an inducement to stay in the profession rather than to quit, and generates high morale, all of which are conducive to an efficient profession. It is therefore useful to consider the remuneration received by teachers in Japan as compared with that in other countries. The relevant information has been collected for thirteen economically advanced nations by Passow, Noah, Eckstein and Mallea (1976). Three measures of teachers' pay were calculated and the results are shown as a whole in Table 7.4.

Firstly, data were presented on the pay of primary school teachers calculated as a percentage of the average of that of minor white collar workers in the respective countries. These percentages run from 189

Table 7.4   Indices of teachers' pay in 13 countries

Country	Primary	Secondary	All
Australia	119	58	115
Belgium	100	–	73
England	86	51	80
Finland	122	65	234
Germany FR	120	38	213
Hungary	91	–	98
Italy	67	42	100
Japan	86	57	78
Netherlands	111	27	126
New Zealand	189	60	125
Scotland	–	–	120
Sweden	118	100	235
USA	128	–	125

Source: Passow *et al*. (1976)

per cent in New Zealand, where primary school teachers are exceptionally well paid, to 67 per cent in Italy, where their pay is poor. Japanese primary school teachers are evidently poorly paid, since the Japanese come second from bottom among the advanced nations on this measure at 86 per cent of the average pay of minor white collar workers. Secondly, secondary teachers' pay was calculated as a percentage of the pay of major professional workers. Here teachers in Sweden do best at 100 per cent (that is, precisely the average) and those in The Netherlands worst at 27 per cent. Japanese secondary teachers are about average among this set of nations. Thirdly, data were presented for the average of primary and secondary teachers' pay as a percentage of average earnings in manufacturing industry. It was found that there is a considerable range from the most generous payments in Sweden and Finland (235 and 234 per cent of average earnings) to the least generous in Japan and Belgium (78 and 73 per cent of average earnings).

The overall picture indicated by these results is that Japanese teachers are paid quite poorly or at best about average, as compared with those in other economically advanced nations. English teachers are also paid relatively poorly. American teachers, on the other hand, are paid relatively well, especially primary school teachers. Passow *et al.* (1976) have calculated the correlations between teachers' remuneration and children's educational achievement in the international science study, and these correlations are shown in Table 7.5. None of them is statistically significant.

Table 7.5 Correlations between indices of teachers' pay and children's science attainment scores

	10-year-olds Science	14-year-olds Science
Primary Teachers' Pay	.07	–
Secondary Teachers' Pay	–	.35
Primary and Secondary Teachers' Pay	.02	.08

Source: Passow *et al.* (1976)

The first international study of achievement in mathematics also gave the correlation between the scores of 13-year-olds and secondary schools teachers' salaries (Husen, 1967). The correlation of -0.87 is statistically significant, indicating that in countries where teachers are poorly paid achievement is higher than in countries where teachers are well paid. For this calculation teachers' salaries in different countries were calculated in US dollars and thus were expressed in absolute terms rather than relative to other occupations in the same country, as in the earlier comparisons in this section. The high negative correlation reflects primarily the fact that American teachers were exceptionally well paid in absolute terms in the 1960s and Japanese teachers poorly paid, yet Japanese children performed considerably better than American children. This high negative correlation should probably not be interpreted as indicating that there is a direct negative causal relationship in the sense that poorly paid teachers actually produce better academic results than the highly paid. Nevertheless, the evidence presented in this section makes it difficult to avoid the conclusion that the level of teachers' remuneration in different countries has no effect on the educational standards achieved by children.

7.8 FINANCIAL RESOURCES FOR SCHOOLS

It is widely believed that the financial resource available to schools are an important determinant of pupils' educational attainment. Greater financial resources make it possible to increase the numbers of teachers and so provide smaller classes, to attract a better quality of recruit into the teaching profession, and to improve school buildings, libraries, laboratories and other physical conditions. It is this belief that has fuelled the large increases in public expenditures on education which have taken place in all economically advanced nations since the end of the Second World War. However, contrary to this widely held expectation, it was shown in the last section that national differences in educational achievement are negatively related to teachers' pay in absolute terms and are independent of teachers' pay relative to that of other occupations in the same country. Teachers' pay is everywhere the largest single item in educational expenditure and hence these data suggest that national differences in educational expenditures are unlikely to be related to children's educational standards.

The first evidence on overall expenditures on education in different countries and the relation of these to educational standards was collected in the 1960s in the first international study of achievement in mathematics (Husen, 1967). The expenditures per pupil in different

Table 7.6   Expenditure per pupil in US dollars for 13-year-olds, 18-year-old mathematician specialists and 18-year-old non-mathematicians

	Expenditures per pupil		
	13-year-olds	*18 Ms*	*18 N-Ms*
Australia	182	194	–
England	208	237	235
Finland	148	187	194
France	197	308	288
Germany FR	–	284	–
Japan	53	80	65
Netherlands	154	357	356
Scotland	294	280	274
Sweden	227	263	265
United States	214	270	270
Correlations with achievement	−.85*	−.53	−.87*

*Asterisked correlations are statistically significant at the 5 per cent level
Source: Husen (1967)

countries were calculated for the 13-year-olds, 18-year-old mathematics specialists and 18-year-old non-specialists. These expenditures were expressed in US dollars and are thus the absolute expenditures in the respective countries. These expenditures are shown in Table 7.6. It will be seen that these expenditures are very low in Japan, where they are between one quarter and one third of those in the West. The correlations between these expenditures and the scores in the mathematics tests are given in the bottom row of the table. It will be seen that all three are negative and high, and that two of these are statistically significant, indicating strong inverse associations between national expenditures and academic standards.

More recent data on public expenditures on education, calculated as a proportion of gross national product (GNP), have been collected for the year 1980 by the statistical secretariat of the United Nations Organisation. These percentages are shown in Table 7.7. The figures displayed in this table suggest that the nations fall into two broad groups. There are seven high spending nations which devote between 7.0 and 9.5 per cent of their gross national product to education. These comprise The Netherlands, the Scandinavian countries, the United States, Canada and Ireland. The last of these is something of a special case because of the large child population and relatively low gross

Table 7.7   Public expenditure on education as a percentage of gross national product (GNP) in the 18 economically advanced western nations for the year 1980

High Spenders	Percent GNP	Low Spenders	Percent GNP
Sweden	9.5	Britain	5.8
Norway	9.0	Japan	5.8
Netherlands	8.4	Finland	5.7
Canada	7.7	Austria	5.6
Denmark	7.0	New Zealand	5.6
Ireland	7.0	Italy	5.1
United States	7.0	France	5.0
Belgium	6.0	Switzerland	5.0
Australia	5.9	West Germany	4.7

Source: United Nations Demographic Yearbook (1983)

national product. The second group consists of eleven low spending nations which devote between 4.7 and 6.0 per cent of their gross national product to public expenditure on education. It will be seen that Japan falls into this low spending group. Again, the conclusion has to be drawn that the high educational standards in Japan are not apparently achieved through exceptionally high public expenditure.

7.9 TEACHER-PUPIL RATIOS AND THE SIZE OF CLASSES

Of all the benefits which are generally believed to accrue from increases in expenditure on education, the one to which most importance is usually attached is the reduction in the size of classes. With smaller classes the teachers can give children more individual attention and this must surely raise the efficiency of instruction and result in better learning. In spite of this widespread belief, the results of research on this question have almost invariably shown no relationship, or at best very little, between the educational attainment of pupils and class size or teacher/pupil ratios. In Britain the researchers for the National Children's Bureau's longitudinal study of all the babies born in Britain in the week 3–9 March 1958 found that class size was related positively to the level of attainment reached by the children in reading and mathematics at the age of sixteen, that is, pupils in larger classes did better. This is a not uncommon finding in studies of this kind and probably reflects a tendency of teachers to put backward children into smaller classes, but it does nevertheless place a strong question mark over the supposed beneficial effects of small classes (Fogelman, 1983, p. 256).

In the United States numerous studies of the relation of class size to educational achievement have been reviewed by Glass and Smith (1978). They concluded that there is no relationship between the two. Walberg (1984) also reviews studies in this area and gives a median correlation of − 0.09 for the relationship between class size and pupil attainment, which should be considered as virtually negligible. A number of studies in Sweden and elsewhere have been summarised by Marklund (1962), who likewise found no relationship between class size and pupil attainment.

It is nevertheless interesting to consider national differences in class size and teacher/pupil ratios, and in particular how Japanese schools compare in an international context in this respect with those in the West. The first international study of mathematics achievement gave data on class sizes for a number of economically advanced countries for 13-year-olds, 18-year-old mathematics specialists and 18-year-old mathematics non-specialists (Husen, 1967). The mathematics mean scores for the countries have been given in Tables 2.1 and 2.2, and it will be recalled that Japanese children obtained the highest mean scores in all three groups. Table 7.8 gives the figures for the same countries for average class sizes. It will be seen that class sizes are exceptionally large in Japan. The average class size for 18-year-old mathematics specialist pupils in Japan was 41, as compared with 12 in England and 21 in the United States. In all comparisons for all three age groups Japan had by far the largest classes. The correlations across countries have been calculated and are given in the bottom row of Table 7.8. All three correlations are positive, and thus tend to show that large classes are associated with high levels of achievement across countries. This does not of course indicate that the effect is causal, but it does suggest that small classes do little to raise educational standards and thereby confirms the numerous studies within countries to which reference has been made above.

Similar data were collated in the international study of science achievement (Comber and Keeves, 1973). The means for 10-year-olds and 14-year-olds for children from the various countries on the science tests have been given in Table 2.3. Staff/pupil ratios for the same pupils arc given in columns 4 and 5 of Table 7.8. Here it will be noted that the Japanese teacher/pupil ratio of 27.4 for 10-year-olds is about average among this set of economically advanced nations; but

Table 7.8 Class sizes and teacher–pupil ratios in various countries

| | Class Size | | | Teacher–Pupil Ratios Science | |
	Maths 18MS	18 N-M	13 yr	10 yr	14 yr
Australia	22	–	36	–	19.3
Belgium	19	24	24	20.1	13.3
England	12	22	30	28.4	18.0
Finland	23	25	30	18.7	20.2
France	26	36	29	–	–
Germany FR	14	15	–	33.2	27.4
Hungary	–	–	–	20.1	20.3
Israel	20	–	–	–	–
Italy	–	–	–	19.6	15.6
Japan	41	41	41	27.4	21.9
Netherlands	19	12	25	30.5	17.8
New Zealand	–	–	–	–	22.2
Scotland	21	22	30	27.4	17.1
Sweden	21	27	26	17.1	14.2
USA	21	26	29	25.5	19.7
Correlations with achievement	.39	.62*	.36	-.28	.59*

Notes: Correlations with pupils' mathematics and science achievement in bottom row. Asterisks denote statistical significance at the 5 per cent level
Source: Husen (1967); Comber and Keeves (1973)

for 14-year-olds the Japanese teacher/pupil ratios are relatively unfavourable and only surpassed by West Germany and New Zealand. The correlations between the teacher/pupil ratios for science and pupil attainment for 14-year-olds is $+0.59$ and is statistically significant, indicating that high teacher/pupil ratios are significantly associated with high levels of attainment in this group of nations. It may be thought that the data shown in Table 7.8 for class size and teacher/pupil ratios do not seem entirely consistent across countries. It appears that class sizes in Japan are very large by international comparison, but the teacher/pupil ratios, although on the high side, are broadly comparable to those in other countries. The reason for this is the practice in Japan whereby teachers tend to spend less hours in the classroom and more time in preparation and marking. When they are in the classroom Japanese teachers typically teach large classes of 40 or even 50 children. It may be that this is a more cost-effective use of teachers' time and energies than the practice in Western countries in which teachers spend more time in the classroom teaching smaller numbers. Whether or not this is the case, the review in this section, taken as a whole, seems to indicate fairly conclusively that in the international context large classes tend to be associated with higher educational standards. Certainly so far as Japan is concerned classes are much larger than those generally present in the West.

7.10 INSTRUCTION TIME: SCHOOL WORK AND HOMEWORK

The amount of time children devote to their school work as a determinant of their standards of achievement was first formalised in a model of educational achievement constructed in the early 1960s by Carroll (1963). This proposition clearly has a strong appeal to common sense. If it were not correct it is arguable that there would be no point in any school work or homework, and this is a position which few have been willing to adopt. Furthermore, since Carroll's formulation of the hypothesis there have been a number of studies of the relation of instruction time to educational achievement which have demonstrated the expected relationship. 31 studies on this subject have been synthesised by Parkerson, Schiller, Lomax and Walberg (1984), who give a median correlation of 0.40 between the quantity of instruction and educational achievement.

With regard to the amount of instruction time devoted to school work in Japan as compared with other economically advanced nations, undoubtedly the most striking feature of Japanese schooling is the length of the school year. Japanese schools are required by law to provide instruction for 240 days per year (Cummings, 1980; Karweit, 1985). This compares with a working school year of approximately 180 days in Britain and the United States and a norm of around 180 to 200 working days in advanced Western nations as a whole. Some useful figures for the length of the school year in secondary schools (those for primary schools are broadly similar) in fifteen advanced nations have been collected by Passow *et al.* (1976), and these are shown in the first column of Table 7.9 (these authors made a slip in the figures they gave for Japan; the correct figure of 240 days is given in the table). It will be seen that Japanese school children work the longest school year among this set of nations and that their working year is greater by one third than that in Britain and the United States.

The amount of instruction time which children in different countries devote to school work is quite a complicated matter, and the estimation of it contains pitfalls which not all investigators have negotiated successfully. In some cases investigators have used hours studied per week as their measure of instruction time. This is clearly unsatisfactory in view of the considerable differences in the number of weeks worked per year by school children in different countries. It is also desirable to consider the time devoted to particular academic subjects in relation to standards achieved in those subjects, and to take into account homework as well as time spent in school. These figures are best calculated either as yearly hours, or as total hours of schooling over a number of years up to the time of taking the achievement test.

In order to obtain broad orders of magnitude of national differences in instruction time in fifteen advanced nations, Table 7.9 presents in columns 1, 2 and 3 the number of working days in the secondary school year, the length of the working day, and the number of hours worked per year. These figures are calculated from Passow *et al.* (1976), and relate to total instruction time in schools, irrespective of the subjects studied (closely similar figures are given by Husen, 1967). It will be noted that although Japanese children work an exceptionally long school year, their working day is relatively short. It consists of 4.6 hours as compared with 5.0 hours in both Britain and the United States and between 5 and 6 hours in most other countries. The relatively short working day in Japan partially offsets the long working year, but the overall figure for instruction hours per year in Japanese secondary

Table 7.9   Various measures of time devoted to school work in different countries

Country	Days per year	Hours per day	Hours per year	Maths Homework Hours per year	Hours of Science Instruction	
					10 yr	14 yr
Australia	200	5.4	1080	88	200	641
Belgium	200	5.6	1120	144	0	218
England	180	5.0	900	77	135	648
Finland	194	6.0	1164	108	408	1014
France	155	5.0	775	105	294	553
Germany FR	230	4.0	920	156		
Hungary	200	5.0	1000		202	757
Israel	210	5.0	1050	185	315	756
Italy	195	5.8	1131		210	466
Japan	240	4.6	1104	144	336	870
Netherlands	200	5.6	1120	104	61	515
New Zealand	195	5.4	1053		406	734
Scotland	200	5.4	1080	92	154	472
Sweden	180	6.0	1080	68	496	1089
USA	180	5.0	900	112	252	720
Correlations with achievement				.44	.63*	.52

Sources: Columns 1, 2 and 3: secondary school days per year, hours per day and hours per year from Passow (1976), column 4, 13-year-olds maths homework per year calculated from figures given by Husen (1967, vol. 2, p. 187); columns 5 and 6: total hours of science instruction by ages 10 and 14, Japanese figures corrected, from Passow (1976)

schools (1104 hours) remains some 22 per cent higher than those in Britain and the United States. Furthermore, it seems probable that the Japanese system of a relatively short working day spread over a greater number of days is more efficient, because of smaller fatigue effects, than the alternative arrangement of a longer working day concentrated into a smaller number of days.

So much for the broad picture of working practices in Japanese schools. For a more refined analysis it is necessary to examine instruction time in particular subjects in relation to standards of educational achievement in those subjects. The first international study of achievement in mathematics did not give data for the hours per year devoted to the study of mathematics, but it did give data for the hours per year of mathematics homework. These data are given in column 4 of Table 7.9. It will be seen that the amount of mathematics homework done by Japanese secondary school children is high by international comparison. It is almost double that in England and about a third more than that in the United States. The correlation between the amount of mathematics homework done per year and mathematics achievement is $+0.44$, but this is not statistically significant with this number of countries.

In the case of national differences in instruction time in science, data have been collected by Passow, Noah, Eckstein and Mallea (1976) for the total number of hours of instruction received by children in the different countries by the time they took the tests at the ages of ten and fourteen years. This measure takes into account the different ages at which children begin compulsory education. Among this set of advanced nations only England, Scotland and Israel require children to attend school at the age of five. The other countries require children to start school at the age of six, except for Finland, Sweden and the Netherlands which do not require children to attend school until the age of seven. Clearly, therefore, these differences in starting ages entail quite considerable differences in the amount of schooling children have received by the ages of ten and fourteen. Nevertheless, it is unlikely that the science learned by 5-year-olds in England, Scotland and Israel will be of much benefit to them for the tests they take at the ages of ten and fourteen and the wisdom of selecting figures for total hours of instruction up to the time of taking the tests has to be questioned.

The calculations made by Passow *et al.* for the numbers of hours of schooling in the various countries are set out in column 5 and 6 of Table 7.9. It will be seen that Japanese children have received quite substantially more schooling in science by the ages of ten and fourteen years than children in either England or the United States, although children in Finland and Sweden receive even more hours of instruction in science. (The figures for Japanese children given in Table 7.9 are greater than those given by Passow *et al*. because of an error made by these authors in the length of the Japanese school year.) The correlation between national science instruction hours by the age of ten years and science achievement mean scores given by Comber and Keeves (1973) is 0.63 and is statistically significant at the 5 per cent level; at age fourteen the correlation is 0.52 (a correlation of 0.53 is statistically significant on this number of cases). Taking the data displayed in Table 7.9 as a whole, we note three substantial correlations between the amount of instruction time and educational achievement across this set of advanced nations.

The relatively large amount of time devoted to schooling by Japanese children shown in these data has been confirmed in the more recent studies of primary schooling in the Minneapolis-Sendai study carried out by Stevenson (1983) and his collaborators (Stigler, Lee, Lucker and Stevenson, 1982). They estimated that among 10-year-olds Japanese children spent 33 hours per week in academic work as compared with 20 hours for American children. Taking into account the greater length of the school year in Japan, it can be calculated that Japanese children work a 1584 hour year and American children a 720 hour year – less than half. These figures are for academic work as a whole. For mathematics it was found that at both the 6- and 10-year-old levels Japanese children spent more of their time on mathematics than American children (23 per cent in Sendai as against 17 per cent in Minneapolis).

The respective figures are shown in Table 7.10, which gives in addition the same data for Taipei which were also collected in this study. In the third row of this table are given figures for the three cities for 10-year-olds for hours spent on learning mathematics in school. It will be seen here that Japanese children spent approaching three times as much time on mathematics as American children, and Taiwanese children spend even more.

Even these striking differences do not take into account the amount of mathematics homework done by children in these three countries. The authors give this in minutes per week as 79 for the United States and 233 for Japan for 6-year-olds; and as 256 (United States) and 368 (Japan) for 10-year-olds. The full data are given in Table 7.10. These figures do not take into account the longer working year in Japan,

Table 7.10 Time spent on mathematics, given as percentages of total instruction time, as hours per annum and as minutes per week homework

Age	Measure	Minneapolis	Sendai	Taipei
6 yrs	Percentage time	14	25	17
10 yrs	Percentage time	17	23	28
10 yrs	Hours p. annum	122	332	538
6 yrs	Homework pw	79	233	496
10 yrs	Homework pw	256	368	771

Source: Stigler, Lee, Lucker and Stevenson, 1982

which increases further the Japanese advantage. Thus, taking instruction time and homework together, it is clear that Japanese children at the primary school stage devote substantially greater time to learning mathematics than American children. Stevenson and his colleagues argue that the greater teaching input and instruction time in Japan (and also in Taiwan) makes a substantial contribution to the high standards of mathematics achievement of young Japanese children. It seems clear that they have a good case.

Finally, we consider the time devoted to school work by Japanese adolescents at the senior secondary school stage of their education. Here Japanese adolescents continue to work a longer school year than in Britain, the United States (240 days as against 180 days) and generally elsewhere in Western countries. But at this stage, as adolescents become more self-motivated, it may well be that the differences in the amount of homework undertaken voluntarily, or at least semi-voluntarily, make the more decisive contribution to national differences in educational achievement. Some striking evidence on the amount of homework done by Japanese adolescents in the 16- to 18-year-old age range has been collected by Walberg, Harnisch and Tsai (1985). It will be recalled that in this study comparing standards in mathematics in Japan and Illinois these authors found that Japanese 16- to 18-year-olds scored approximately two standard deviations above those in the United States. In examining the amount of homework done, the authors estimated this at 4.5 hours per week in the United States and 60 hours per week in Japan. It is difficult to dispute the authors' conclusion that this massive difference in the amount of homework undertaken must be a significant factor in the high educational standards achieved by Japanese adolescents.

Thus we have seen that from the early years of primary school through to the early years of secondary school and on to the 16- to 18-year-old stage, Japanese children and adolescents spend more time on their education than is typically the case in the advanced Western nations. As compared with Britain and the United States, Japanese children in primary school and early secondary school are devoting about 25 to 50 per cent more time both to school work and to homework, while among 16- to 18-year-olds the amount of time Japanese adolescents spend on homework is apparently some thirteen times greater than that of American adolescents. Even these figures do not take account of the extensive supplementary schooling in Japan, known as the *juku*, which operate alongside the ordinary school system by providing extra education in the evenings and holidays and are attended by approximately half of Japanese children. The additional schooling provided by the *juku* increases still further the time devoted to education by Japanese children. But even discounting the *juku*, it is clear that Japanese children and adolescents devote substantially more time to education than Western children generally. It seems difficult to dispute the conclusion that this must be a significant factor in the high standards of educational achievement in Japan.

7.11 CONCLUSIONS

This chapter begins by noting the high level of professionalism of Japanese teachers and the important contribution which this must make to Japanese educational standards. It is considered that three factors are responsible for this high level of professionalism. The first is the detailed specification of the curriculum by government, which provides a sense of direction and a discipline for Japanese teachers that is lacking in Britain and the United States.

The second is the competition between Japanese high schools for public esteem secured through good examination results. This mobilises the motives of competitiveness and self-esteem among Japanese teachers and provides an incentive to teach efficiently in order to maintain the public reputation of the school. The third is the large private sector in Japanese education. The efficiency of the private schools can be understood as a special case of the general principle that goods and services provided by private competing suppliers are produced more efficiently than those provided by public monopolies.

Evidence is reviewed next on Japanese teachers' ability, training, and remuneration, and it is seen that in none of these respects do Japanese teachers enjoy any advantage over those generally prevailing in the West. The relatively modest pay received by Japanese teachers leads to further consideration of the financial resources available to Japanese schools. It is shown that Japanese schools do not receive greater financial support from government and that, on the contrary, the funding of schools is quite low in Japan. This is reflected in the size of classes in Japan, which are typically very large compared to those in the West. All these are important negative conclusions.

Considered finally is the amount of time Japanese school children devote to their academic work. It is noted that the Japanese school year of 240 working days is substantially longer than the 180 days normally worked in Britain and the United States. It is proposed that Japanese children must secure a substantial advantage from the greater amount of time they devote to their education.

8 Four Lessons for the West

In this concluding chapter we consider what lessons the West can learn from education in Japan, the high educational standards of Japanese children, and the ways in which these high standards are achieved. There are two broad levels at which the Japanese experience is instructive. Firstly, the high Japanese educational standards appear to be attributable to the operation in Japan of certain general principles for securing efficiency. Secondly, there is the detailed way in which these principles are made effective. These details provide a useful model of how a highly efficient education system works in practice, although it is not suggested that the Western nations should necessarily attempt to copy the Japanese system in every particular. It may be possible to realise the underlying principles in different ways.

The reader who has followed the argument to this point will have discerned that there are four important principles to be learned from Japanese education. The first of these is negative, and is that the high educational standards of Japan are achieved without greater financial resources than those available in the West. The remaining three principles are positive, and are that the major factors responsible for the high educational standards in Japan lie, firstly, in the strong incentives for school children to undertake academic work: secondly, in the length of the school year, and thirdly in the strong incentives for teachers to work efficiently. In this final chapter we consider the feasibility of applying these principles to the school systems of the West.

8.1 INCENTIVES FOR SCHOOL CHILDREN

It was argued in detail in Chapter 5 that the first principle responsible for the high educational standards of Japanese school children lies in the powerful incentives for academic work. The most important of these incentives are the entrance examinations for senior high schools taken at the age of fourteen, and for universities and colleges taken by large numbers of young Japanese at the age of seventeen plus. These incentives act as powerful motivators for academic work for the two or three year periods leading up to the examinations.

The question of incentives for school children to do academic work has received very little consideration by educationists, social scientists and politicians in Britain and the United States. Standard textbooks of education, educational psychology and educational sociology typically give no discussion of incentives and the part they might play in the motivation of school children. This omission is all the more curious because in the adult world of work the importance of incentives is widely acknowledged. Industrial psychologists and sociologists have investigated thoroughly the effectiveness of incentives of various kinds on workers' outputs and productivity, and the motivating function of incentives normally receives extensive coverage in textbooks on industrial psychology and sociology.

It is not only social scientists who have neglected to consider the role of incentives for the work motivation of school children. Government commissions set up to consider the unsatisfactory state of education have also failed to appreciate the significance of incentives. For instance, the United States Education Commission's report, *Action for Excellence: A Comprehensive Plan to Improve our Nation's Schools* (1983), put forward 30 recommendations for how the standards of American education should be raised. These recommendations consist almost entirely of exhortations, for example, 'Business leaders, labor leaders, and members of the professions should become more active in education'. In Britain the Bullock Commission, which was set up in the early 1970s to consider the problem of the poor standards of literacy of large numbers of school leavers, recommended the establishment of a national system for monitoring standards, the appointment of educational advisers for teachers, the appointment of additional staff for teaching backward readers, the setting up of a national network of reading clinics, and the foundation of a national centre for research on language education (Bullock, 1975). In neither of these American or British commissions was any consideration given to the question of what incentives might be provided for school children to learn, or for teachers to increase their teaching efficiency.

The principal lesson from Japan in regard to incentives for school children is that the most powerful incentives are examinations, which it is important for them to pass. These examinations can be of two kinds. Firstly, there is the Japanese model of entrance examinations to schools and universities. The second is public examinations of the type of the British GCE and CSE examinations. These act as incentives because the certificates awarded for passing these examinations are required .as credentials by employers, universities and other institutions of tertiary education.

Of these two alternative forms of examination, the Japanese system would be the more difficult to introduce in the West. To introduce a 'fourteen plus' examination for hierarchically ranked senior high schools would entail a radical reorganisation of the school system. Firstly, secondary schooling would have to be broken into two stages, as in Japan, in order to provide entrance examinations to new schools taken at the age of fourteen or thereabouts. Secondly, it would be necessary to establish large numbers of private schools such as exist in Japan.

The Japanese private senior high schools are obliged to compete because their existence depends on competitive success, and the large numbers of these private high schools force the public schools to compete as well. In a wholly public system it would be difficult to get schools to compete and form a status hierarchy. Education officials and the professional associations of teachers invariably prefer to minimise competition to vanishing point and promote uniformity between institutions. For these reasons it is considered that the Japanese model of competitive examinations for hierarchically ranked senior high schools would be politically difficult to introduce in the West.

The alternative form of examination incentive for teenagers in mid-adolescence is the public examination of which the British GCE and CSE are the leading exemplars. This is undoubtedly an effective incentive for those adolescents who take these public examinations seriously, because they know their future careers depend on their obtaining the certificates awarded to successful candidates. The weakness of these British public examinations is that only about half of the age cohorts do take these examinations seriously. This weakness is relatively easily remedied and consists of restructuring the examination in such a way that it is taken by virtually all adolescents, and the certificate awarded for passing rapidly becomes a credential demanded by the great majority of employers. Restructuring along these lines has already been undertaken by the British government and is scheduled for introduction in 1988. The British experience has been that it is possible to introduce a public examination of this kind for all adolescents with relatively little opposition.

In the United States there has been no tradition of public examinations until the introduction, in the 1970s, of minimum competence tests in most of the American states. The weakness of these tests is that they only provide a challenge to the least able adolescents who find them difficult. Nevertheless, it should be relatively straightforward to develop these tests further on the lines of the British model of public examinations with around half a dozen grades of pass set at different levels of difficulty. These would provide for all American adolescents the incentives which are so conspicuously lacking in American education.

A debatable further question is whether the public examinations of the British type for 16-year-olds could usefully be provided at some earlier stage of schooling, say for 10- or 11-year-olds. A proposal of this kind has been made by Cox and Boyson (1977). The arguments for such an examination are as follows. Firstly, public examinations exert motivating effects on the academic work efforts of school children for the preceding two or three years. It could not be expected that public examinations taken at the age of sixteen would have any motivating effects on children at primary schools. An examination for 10- to 11-year-olds, taken at the end of the last year of primary school, would fulfil this function. Secondly, public examinations serve a socialising purpose through their reward for achievement. The concentration of children's work efforts towards the objective of doing well in a primary school leaving examination would make a contribution to the development of the work ethic. Thirdly, such an examination would identify children who had failed to learn to read and perform simple calculations. There is no doubt that very large numbers of children fail to acquire these important basic skills at their primary schools in both Britain and the United States. In Britain, Cox and Boyson (1977) present evidence that approximately 25 per cent of children leave their primary schools deficient in these skills, and the figure in the United States is certainly at least as high as this (Lerner, 1983; Education Commission of the States, 1983). A public examination at the end of the primary school stage would focus attention on these children and would lead to corrective tuition, so that they would not continue to drift through secondary school still illiterate and innumerate.

Fourthly, public examinations serve as a motivator for teachers to teach efficiently as well as for children. Primary school teachers in Britain and the United States have little external incentive to teach efficiently and there is little doubt that this is a contributory cause of the large numbers of children who leave primary school unable to read or do simple arithmetical calculations (see, for example, Cockcroft, 1982). The performance of children in public examinations would constitute a useful measure of the teaching efficiency of schools and would act as a motivator for teachers to ensure that adequate standards were being achieved.

8.2 SOME POSSIBLE COSTS OF THE JAPANESE SYSTEM

There will no doubt be some who will suspect that the high educational standards in Japan entail certain costs. There are probably three of these that will be foremost in the minds of many readers. These are that the pressures to which Japanese school children are subjected may generate psychological maladjustment, may foster conformity and memorisation at the expense of creativity and may have adverse effects on less able children. In this section we consider the degree to which these three possible costs may be present in Japanese education.

(a) Psychological Maladjustment

It may be supposed that the Japanese system is too competitive and is likely to generate a high level of psychological stress and maladjustment among Japanese school children. This possibility can be examined by comparison of the scores on questionnaire measures of anxiety of Japanese children compared with those in the West. A study of this kind comparing the responses of Japanese and British children on Eysenck's neuroticism questionnaire, a self-rating measure of symptoms and feelings of anxiety and stress, found no differences between children aged ten to fifteen years from the two countries (Iwawaki, Eysenck and Eysenck, 1980).

It is also possible to take suicide rates as an index of extreme reaction to stress. The position here is that among economically developed nations suicide rates in Japan tend to be high among all age groups, but not exceptionally so. Suicide rates in Japan are no higher than those in West Germany, Denmark, Austria or Hungary (Lynn, 1982c) and this is the case for juvenile suicide rates as well as for overall suicide rates. This question has been fully discussed by Rohlen (1983), who concludes that although some school children in Japan are driven to suicide by examination stress, this is also the case in other countries and the proportion is no greater in Japan than in many Western nations.

(b) Conformity versus Creativity

A second cost which has sometimes been suggested of Japanese education is that the emphasis placed on achievement in examinations fosters conformity, cramming for facts and the learning of routine reasoning skills at the expense of the development of creativity. This line of criticism points out that Japanese intellectual creativity at the higher level, as indexed by the award of Nobel prizes for science, is quite weak in Japan as compared with that in the West. Critics of this kind further suggest that the indisputable Japanese economic achievements since the end of World War Two have typically been secured through efficient exploitation and application of discoveries made by scientists in the West. To some extent the Japanese have themselves accepted this criticism, and in the early 1980s the Japanese Prime Minister established a commission to consider how greater creativity could be developed in Japanese schools and universities.

There are several points to be made about this criticism of Japanese education. Firstly, it is sometimes argued that emphasis on the acquisition of facts and routine reasoning procedures, such as those used in mathematics, have an inhibiting effect on creativity. It is doubtful whether this is correct. The psychological processes involved in high level creative thought were described introspectively in a classical analysis by the French mathematician Poincaré (1913). His conclusion was that the first essential is to attain complete mastery of the relevant facts. The creative element is to reorganise the facts, but this cannot be achieved unless the facts themselves are well known. A more contemporary analysis which reaches the same conclusion has been given by De Bono (1977). A mastery of existing knowledge and creative thinking are two complementary processes in creative intellectual achievement.

Secondly, Japanese children are at least as strong on the more creative tasks tested in the international achievement investigations as on the more factual tasks. For instance, in the first international study of mathematics, Japanese children did as well in the tests of algebra, geometry and verbal problems as they did in the more routine tests of arithmetical computations (Husen, 1967, p. 32). These results suggest that the emphasis on academic achievement in Japan does not impair the more creative thought processes, at least to the extent that these are measured by problem solving tests.

Thirdly, the relatively weak Japanese record in high level creative science as indexed by Nobel prize awards can be quite straightforwardly explained as largely due to the small Japanese investment of ability, effort and financial resources in pure science. Japanese students with scientific interests and talents generally study engineering at university and only study pure science in relatively small numbers. Comparisons with Britain and the United States are shown in Table 8.1. The very low numbers of Japanese students specialising in science and the large numbers in engineering must go a long way towards explaining the relatively low level of Japanese achievement in pure science as contrasted with the excellence of Japanese achievements in engineering.

Table 8.1   Proportions of students studying science and engineering in 1970

	Science	*Engineering*
Japan	3.1	21.1
Britain	24.5	17.7
United States	9.3	6.0

Source: Mombusho (1975)

(c) Incentives for Less Able Children

A third possible cost in Japanese education concerns its effects on less able pupils. We have seen that in Japan the incentives and rewards for academic success are exceptionally strong. The other side of the coin is that the penalties for failure are also strong. It may be considered that although a system of this kind would be effective in generating motivation for academic achievement for the more able, for whom academic success comes relatively easily, it would have depressing effects on the less able, who would be likely to give up and drop out of the system. Arguments of this kind played an important part in the movement to abolish the grammar schools in Britain. No-one disputed that the grammar schools provided a good education for the more gifted children who were able to get into them. It was their depressing effects on the less able children who failed to get into them that was one of the principal criticisms of the grammar schools.

The evidence on this point, however, suggests that the Japanese system does not generate the demoralising effects on the less able that might be anticipated. For quantitative evidence on this point it is only necessary to consider the standard deviations of the educational achievement test scores for various nations, given in detail in Chapter 2. The Japanese standard deviations are not in general particularly large by international comparison. This shows that the high standards are present throughout the whole range of ability, at the top, in the middle and at the bottom. It will be recalled also that in the Stevenson (1983) study of achievement in mathematics in schools in Minneapolis and Sendai, the school with the lowest mean score in Sendai scored higher than the best school in Minneapolis. Here is further evidence that the academic standards of all children are high in Japan, not merely those of some proportion of more able children who respond well to the competitive and demanding system.

The principal way in which the Japanese system prevents demoralisation among the less able is in the breaking of secondary education into the two stages of the junior and senior high schools. The effect of this is that young adolescents of all ability levels at junior high school have the incentive of working to secure entry to a good senior high school. In this way the Japanese system succeeds in avoiding the undoubtedly demoralising effect that irremediable assignment to an inferior secondary school at a relatively young age undoubtedly used to have on many less able adolescents in selective European systems, until these were comprehensivised in the 1960s and 1970s.

8.3 LENGTH OF THE SCHOOL YEAR

It was argued in Chapter 7 that a second major factor responsible for the high educational standards in Japan is the substantially longer school year. Japanese school children work a 240 day year as compared with approximately 180 days in Britain and the United States and a range of 155 days (France) to 230 days (West Germany) in Continental Europe. It is evident that by mid-adolescence Japanese teenagers have had the equivalent of something like three or four years more schooling than their counterparts in Britain and the United States. It seems probable that this advantage is a significant factor in the high educational standards achieved in Japan. It has been found that children forget substantial amounts of their school work over the course of the long summer vacations in the United States (Turner, 1972), and this is avoided in Japan by the shorter holidays. There is furthermore considerable evidence from a number of studies that the quantity of instruction children receive is an important determinant of the amount they learn (Parkerson, Schiller, Lomax and Walberg,

1984). This seems such an obvious proposition, even without its substantial research backing, that it is surprising that there has been so little discussion in Britain and the United States of the possibility of increasing the length of the school year.

So straightforward a solution does this seem to the problem of raising educational standards in the West that a caveat needs to be entered against this apparently simple remedy. It can be confidently predicted that increasing the length of the working school year in Britain and the United States would raise educational standards among the higher ability groups. But among the lower ability groups who are at present leaving in such large numbers without having acquired basic literacy or numeracy, the beneficial effects are much more doubtful. The problem is that so little is being learned at present that increasing the length of the school year would merely add more virtually useless days to those that exist already. In Japan the longer school year secures an advantage because the standards of discipline are so much higher, and the additional days are employed productively. In Britain and the United States it is probable that little would be gained by lengthening the school year so far as the lower ability groups are concerned, without at the same time introducing a number of other measures designed to increase the motivation of children to learn and of teachers to teach efficiently.

8.4 INCENTIVES FOR TEACHER EFFICIENCY *

We turn now to the third major input into the educational standards of children, namely the efficiency of their teachers. It was argued in Chapter 7 that there are three features of education in Japan which sustain teacher efficiency. These are the specification of the curriculum by the Ministry of Education, the competition between high schools and the presence of an extensive private sector. We consider now the feasibility of introducing these incentives in the West.

There is little doubt that maintaining the motivation of teachers for efficient work is a major problem in Britain, the United States and other Western nations. The difficulty lies in the essentially syndicalist organisation of the public schools, in which teachers are in practice largely unaccountable to anyone for the efficiency of their working practices. There are few sanctions for poor work because teachers' efficiency is not carefully appraised and teachers are hardly ever penalised by dismissal or other penalties for inefficient work. There are also relatively weak rewards for good work, again because work is not carefully appraised. Teachers can work within an enormous range of efficiency or inefficiency without either rewards or sanctions. Many teachers are, of course, to some degree motivated intrinsically by a sense of vocation, but the external incentives for teachers to work efficiently are so weak that their working practices are inevitably well below optimum. There has been little understanding among educationists, Ministers of Education and officials responsible for education in Britain and the United States of the weakness of incentives for efficient teaching, and little thought has been given to the problem of how these incentives might be strengthened. Most of the efforts of government towards inproving the quality of teachers' performance have been directed towards attempting to improve teachers' skills rather than their motivation. Thus in Britain the length of training for teachers has been increased from two years in the inter-war and early post-war years to four years, and this training has been integrated with universities in order to make it more rigorous. Refresher courses for teachers have been made widely available and advisers have been appointed to give advice on teaching methods. Similar developments have taken place in the United States, where in a number of states, teachers are required to attend a certain number of lectures per year in order to secure renewal of their contracts or salary increments. None of these measures addresses the problem of increasing the motivation of teachers through sharpening the incentive structure.

Such incentives as do exist for teaching efficiency in Britain and the United States do not operate effectively. The principal discipline for British teachers lies in the reports of the schools' inspectors, who are employed to inspect schools and report on their efficiency. The weaknesses of the inspectorate are that schools are forewarned of the inspectors' visit and can put on a show for the occasion; the inspectors' evaluations are largely inpressionistic rather than being based on objective assessment of the educational standards reached by children; the reports tend to be bland, so that in an analysis of 35 reports on schools Gray and Hannon (1986) could find no thoroughly adverse reports; and even where adverse reports are made few effective sanctions are taken against schools.

Until recently inspectors' reports were kept strictly confidential and this served to reduce still further their effectiveness as a discipline on teachers. This was changed in 1983, when the Secretary of State for Education issued a directive requiring the publication of inspectors' reports. While this is a step in the right direction, it is doubtful whether it will make any great contribution in practice to increasing teachers' accountability to the public. The requirement that inspectors' reports should be published is perhaps most interesting as an indication that government ministers are beginning to be aware of the need to increase the disciplines and incentives for teachers' efficiency. A second indication of this growing awareness is the attempts in recent years to introduce merit awards as financial incentives for good teachers. In Britain the Secretary of State for Education attempted to introduce merit awards during a struggle with the teachers' unions during 1985 and 1986. Similar ideas have been floated in the United States. In Florida a scheme of merit awards for good teachers is planned for implementation in the late 1980s.

While these schemes show some comprehension of the problem of increasing the incentives for teacher efficiency, they cannot be regarded as effective solutions to the problem. There are two difficulties. Firstly, the methods of assessment of teachers' merit will be too rough and ready. They will inevitably depend largely on the recommendations of the head teachers, which will themselves be impressionistic and impossible to compare between one head teacher and another. The working teacher will consequently perceive the possibility of receiving a merit award as substantially governed by chance and by whether he or she is liked by the head teacher and as only weakly contingent on efficient teaching. Secondly, once the awards have been made the incentive to continue working efficiently is removed. What is required for incentives to work is a system which operates continually, like that of the annual bonus payments frequently made to executives in business on the basis of the profits or productivity for which they have been responsible during the preceding year.

There has also been some recognition in recent years among educationists in the United States of the importance of providing stronger incentives for work effort for teachers. Purkey and Smith (1985) discuss this problem. They propose a system whereby schools should be invited to compete for funds to finance special projects designed to improve standards. For instance, schools might design projects for using computers, to reduce dropouts, to improve attendance and behaviour and so forth. These projects would be funded for a three year period and, hopefully, 'competitive grants would both stimulate and support the process of school improvement' (p. 191). Alternatively, schools could be awarded stars after the manner of restaurants in the Michelin guides. These American educationists suggest a three star system. One star would designate acceptable basic standards, two stars would be awarded for a school which set up a 'school improvement committee', 'written plans that address the school's weaknesses' and 'staff development activities'. For the highest accolade of a three star rating schools would have to achieve some unspecified 'predetermined outcomes' for at least two years.

Under such a system, the authors believe, 'it is reasonable to assume that most schools would be under a considerable amount of pressure to move beyond the basic accreditation level' (p. 193). While some reservations may be entertained about how effective the award of these Michelin type stars would be as incentives for teachers, this thoughtful discussion provided by Purkey and Smith does show that some educationists are beginning to understand just how weak the incentives for efficient work for teachers are in the West, and to think about how teacher accountability to the public could be strengthened.

8.5 GOVERNMENT SPECIFICATION OF THE CURRICULUM

The first method by which the efficiency of teachers is maintained in Japan is through the specification of the curriculum by the Japanese Ministry of Education. This sets out in detail the syllabus that teachers are required to teach at each grade and the numbers of hours per year that are to be devoted to each subject.

Japanese schools are monitored by government inspectors to ensure that the Ministry's specifications are being followed. It will be clear that this degree of control acts as a powerful discipline on schools to teach the required curriculum. There is also some element of government control over the curriculum in much of Continental Europe, where governments issue guidelines on the syllabus to be followed in schools, but these are not specified in the same detail as in Japan. Nevertheless, Britain and the United States are exceptional in the autonomy allowed to head teachers and teachers in determining the curriculum that is to be taught in individual schools.

The question to be considered is whether powers to specify the curriculum should be taken by governments in Britain and the United States. There is no doubt that the devolution of responsibility for the curriculum to schools in Britain and the United States entails considerable variation in what is taught in different schools. This variation has been documented for the United States by Berliner

(1985), from whose investigations it appears that in practice even head teachers have little idea of what is actually being taught by individual teachers in their classrooms.

The essential point of principle here is this. It is in the public interest that all children should be taught to read, calculate, comprehend the laws and appreciate the culture of their own and other countries, understand basic scientific principles and so forth. Children need to be educated in order to fulfil their roles as citizens and workers. It is for this reason that governments require children by law to attend school for some ten years. Furthermore, governments attempt to ensure that children are properly taught and employ school inspectors for this purpose. The general principles that governments can legitimately coerce children to attend school and discipline teachers to teach efficiently are therefore well established. The problem in Britain and the United States is that governments' attempts to ensure that children are properly educated are so inadequately realised in practice. An important reason for this is that although governments require children to attend school they do not require teachers to teach a prescribed curriculum.

The principal involved here may be clarified by considering the requirements made by government for the acquisition of a driving licence to drive a car. Governments take the view that it is in the public interest that car drivers should be competent at driving and clearly this view is correct. To ensure this governments require citizens to undergo education in driving and to pass a test of driving proficiency. The curriculum is specified and has to be mastered in order to pass the driving test. However, governments do not specify the amount of time that learner drivers are required to spend in driving school. The requirements made by governments seem to be entirely reasonable for the attainment of the objective of assuring that only competent drivers are permitted to drive on the public highway.

Considered in the light of this model, the policies adopted by British and American governments towards education in schools are less easily justified. Here governments specify the length of time that children must remain in schools, but not what they are taught there. Evidently there is a case that British and American governments have got their priorities wrong, and that the first responsibility of governments is to ensure that children are actually taught the curriculum that it is in the public interest for all children to learn. This is precisely what is ensured in Japan by the detailed government specification of the curriculum.

In addition to the general principle involved, the British and American policies of devolving responsibility for the curriculum to schools have not worked well in practice. The most basic skills of literacy and numeracy are not taught sufficiently thoroughly and far too many adolescents are leaving school after ten or eleven years of compulsory education without being able to read adequately or perform simple calculations (Bullock, 1975; Cockcroft, 1982; Lerner, 1983). Another area where schools in Britain have not in general discharged their responsibilities well is in technical and vocational education. There has been virtually universal agreement for the last century that technical and vocational education in Britain are weak, and it is widely believed that this is an important factor in the poor performance of the British economy since the closing decades of the last century. As long ago as 1884, the Royal Commission on Technical Education drew attention to this problem and urged the strengthening of technical education in Britain. Numerous subsequent commissions and other inquiries continued to draw attention to the weakness of British education in this regard. Precisely 100 years later Hayes, Anderson and Fonda (1984) were able to document that this problem still existed and issued yet another plea for bringing technical education in Britain up to the level of that in other major industrial nations. The failure of British schools to respond to this need, so clearly and frequently voiced over the last 100 years, must call into question whether it has been wise to allow the content of the curriculum to be determined by head teachers.

It is instructive to compare the British experience, so far as education for national economic needs is concerned, with that of Japan. In the early 1960s the Japanese employers' organisation made representations to the Minister of Education to the effect that the standard of mathematics of many school leavers was too low. The Minister took further advice and then responded by raising the standards required at each grade from primary school upwards. The new standards were circulated to all schools and duly taught.

A further aspect of the school curriculum which is interesting to consider is moral education. Throughout the West moral values appear to have declined sharply over the last half century, and there is little doubt that this is one factor in the rising rates of crime which are everywhere a cause of public concern. This raises the question of whether something might not be done to teach and develop moral values in schools. In Britain some Ministers of Education have wished that this could be done, but they have been quite powerless to direct that moral education should be introduced into the school curriculum. In Japan a good deal of thought has been given to the problem of how schools can help to develop and strengthen children's moral values and understanding. In the post-World War Two period Japanese Ministers of Education decided that children's moral understanding can be developed by teaching, by discussion and by practice, as for instance by having children do the cleaning of their own schools, assist in serving and cleaning up after school lunches and so forth, so that they learn to take responsibility and contribute to a common endeavour. These procedures are stipulated by the Ministry of Education as mandatory in Japanese schools. Of course, the very low rates of juvenile crime in Japan as compared with the West cannot with any certainty be attributed to the success of moral education teaching in Japanese schools, but it is surely not implausible to infer that these earnestly executed programmes of moral education have had some beneficial socialising effects.

Any attempt by government in Britain or the United States to specify the content of the school curriculum would no doubt be opposed by teachers' professional associations. The principal grounds for this opposition and justification for the autonomy of teachers and head teachers to determine the school curriculum is that it allows teachers to exercise their professional skills in deciding the subject matter to be taught. The analogy is sometimes drawn with the medical profession. Government does not stipulate in detail how doctors are to treat patients, but leaves such decisions to the professional skills and judgment of doctors. It is argued that similar autonomy should be allowed to teachers. This analogy should be rejected as unpersuasive. The task of the doctor in treating an illness is narrow and specific. The objectives of education are far broader and are too complex to be left to teachers and head teachers to determine. For example, in recent years computers have come to play an important role in economically advanced societies and this prompts the question of whether computer programming and use should be taught in schools. To answer this question requires an assessment of what the demand for computer expertise is likely to be in the future decades, and of what kinds of training in computers would be most usefully taught in schools. Such problems as these are clearly far too complex to be determined by head teachers, who normally know virtually nothing about computers or their use in the world of work and are totally unqualified to make projections about the demand for computer skills in the future. In Japan questions of this kind are determined by panels of experts, among whom teachers and educationists are represented, brought together by the Japanese Minister of Education to thrash these problems out. Even such a panel of experts would have difficulty in assessing future manpower requirements for some decades ahead, but it would surely be better equipped to make judgments of this kind than individual head teachers.

The suggested conclusion to this discussion is that governments have a legitimate interest in ensuring that a certain curriculum is taught in schools; that this is not at present being met sufficiently effectively in Britain and the United States; that the Japanese experience shows that detailed government specification of the curriculum ensures that teaching is more thorough than in the West; and that consideration should be given in the West to the possibility of governments taking greater powers to specify the curriculum. It would not, of course, be necessary for any such specification to be so detailed or comprehensive as in Japan. Western governments might specify a core curriculum that all schools would be required to teach for, say, half of the time, leaving the other half within the discretion of individual schools. This would permit variety and experimentation within a framework of discipline for ensuring that at least the basic skills were properly taught.

8.6 COMPETITION BETWEEN SCHOOLS

It was argued in Chapter 7 that the second important factor responsible for the efficiency of Japanese teachers lies in the competition between schools for examination successes. Competition is particularly strong among the senior high schools. The competition between the high schools in Japan resembles that between firms in the private sector of the economy, and it has a similar stimulating effect on teachers although the objective of the competition is examination results rather than profits or market share. There is very little of this competition between schools in the West, although there is some slight element of it among the independent schools in Britain, where each year the leading academic schools are ranked in the *Times Educational Supplement*, on the basis of the numbers of open scholarships won at Oxford and Cambridge. Appearance in this list, and particularly at the top of it, is considered a distinction for the schools involved. It is a source of pride to the teachers and contributes to their motivation and morale. Nevertheless, this annual ranking of the leading academic schools in Britain receives nothing like the publicity and media interest that the ranking of the senior high schools receives in Japan, and its impact on the motivation of teachers bears no comparison with that generated among Japanese teachers.

The psychological effects of the publication of schools' examination results on teachers is that they act as an incentive for teacher efficiency. This effect is in general poorly understood in the West. In Britain, however, an awareness of it was shown in 1980 by the Secretary of State for Education, when he introduced in the Education Act a directive that all secondary schools should publish information on their recent results in the public examination of GCE and CSE. Although secondary schools have complied with this directive the information is not typically supplied in a particularly helpful form, since the examination passes are usually given without specification of the total numbers of children. Nor have these results been analysed to provide indices of schools' relative efficiency. Nevertheless, after many decades in which the public had no knowledge of the examination results achieved by different schools, the directive contained in the 1980 Education Act does represent a useful start both in the provision of information and in understanding the important functions served by public knowledge of schools' examinations results.

Now that this information on schools' examination achievements is available in Britain, it would be relatively simple to construct indices of schools' efficiency as assessed by their examination results. In the United States there would be some difficulty because there are no public examinations corresponding to the British GCE or the university entrance examinations in Japan which could be used to construct an index of schools' efficiency. Nevertheless, it would be possible to administer academic achievement tests for this purpose.

If the proposal of the American educationists Purkey and Smith (1985) were adopted, to the effect that schools should be awarded stars for efficiency on the same lines as restaurants in the Michelin guides, then the obvious basis on which to award these marks of distinction would surely be the schools' academic achievements as measured by the pupils' successes in examinations, or by some comparable form of academic test.

It may be objected that measuring the efficiency of schools in this way would be unfair to teachers, because children's academic achievements are so strongly determined by their intelligence and family background. It will be said that schools in socially privileged areas will inevitably achieve better examination successes than those in disadvantaged areas. There is of course some truth in this objection, but the problem is not unsuperable. One way of meeting it would be to measure the intelligence of the children and the socioeconomic standing of the schools' catchment areas and adjust for these in the calculation of the schools' academic achievements. The alternative is simply to let schools live with this handicap. It is important to oppose fatalistic attitudes, to insist that schools can do a lot to raise academic standards and should therefore be made responsible for them. In the well-known study of a number of comprehensive schools in London by Rutter, Maughan, Mortimore, Ouston and Smith (1979), it was shown that there were substantial differences between the GCE and CSE results of children from different schools, even when the children were matched for the socioeconomic status of their homes. These differences in academic achievement have to be attributed to differences between schools in teaching effectiveness. We have found similar substantial school effects on educational achievement. In a study of the determinants of GCE and CSE results of approximately 700 adolescents in a town in Northern Ireland, we found that approximately 50 per cent of the variance in examination achievement was attributable to school effects after controlling for both socioeconomic status and intelligence (Lynn, Hampson and Magee, 1983). These results are entirely consistent with the evidence from Japan in indicating that schools can do a great deal by effective teaching to raise standards.

No doubt there will be a number of educationists in the West who will feel unhappy at the prospect of the public ranking of schools in terms of the examination performance of their pupils. If any readers have these reservations they are urged to consider the detailed information which the public can obtain before they buy houses, cars, washing machines and so forth. The public also buy education for their children in their capacity as tax payers, yet they have no way of evaluating the quality of the schools' services. Considered in this light the lack of any public knowledge of the quality of education provided by different schools is surely an anomaly which it is difficult to justify.

8.7 THE PRIVATISATION OF SCHOOLS

It was argued in Chapter 7 that the third factor responsible for the efficiency of Japanese teachers in the senior high schools lies in the large number of private schools. These are forced to be efficient through the necessity of satisfying the parents who pay the fees, and in addition act as an example of efficiency which the public schools are under pressure to emulate. In contrast, schools in the West are largely run as public monopolies. There are of course small numbers of private schools in Britain, the United States and Continental Europe which provide some competition for the public schools. But this competition is not particularly effective, because the high fees of the private schools put them beyond the reach of the great majority of parents. What is required to render competition with the state sector effective is what economists call *the power of exit*, that is, the ability of parents to withdraw their children from the state schools and transfer them into private schools (see Seldon, 1986, for a recent statement of this argument).

Over the last four decades a number of economists and other social scientists have argued that the largely monopolistic provision of education in Britain and the United States has entailed the inefficiencies to which monopolies are typically prone. The argument is that monopolies are insulated from the discipline of competition and the market and that those who work in them tend to deploy their efforts with less energy than those who work in competing institutions. On these grounds it has been proposed that schools should be privatised as a means of increasing their responsiveness to consumer requirements and introducing into education the efficiency generally characteristic of the competitive free enterprise economy. This proposal was set out by Milton Friedman (1962), and has been developed by a number of neo-liberal economists and other social scientists (for example, Maynard, 1975; Marsland, 1981; Everhart, 1982; Dennison, 1984).

These arguments for the privatisation of education have been almost entirely based not on empirical evidence demonstrating the superior efficiency of private schools, but on the general principle that goods and services supplied by monopolies are provided less efficiently than those supplied by competing institutions. The interest of Japanese education from this point of view is that it provides some empirical evidence for the argument that the privatisation of schools would raise standards and also that it provides a unique model of how an education system with a substantial private sector can work in practice.

So far as the argument that the privatisation of schools would raise standards is concerned, ther is no doubt that the private senior high schools in Japan make a significant contribution to the high Japanese educational standards. Many of the private senior high schools are by common consent among the strongest academic schools in the country. Furthermore, as we said in detail in Chapter 3, the private senior high schools have been growing academically stronger over the last two decades at the expense of the public senior high schools. This is likely to happen in a mixed sector of the economy where public and private institutions compete. In these conditions the public institutions will inevitably lose ground because they have less powerful incentives for efficiency, not least of which is the absence of any fear of bankruptcy.

The second lesson from the Japanese experience of the large numbers of private schools concerns the manner in which the privatisation of schools can be promoted. Virtually all those who have considered this question have followed Milton Friedman (1962) in advocating a voucher scheme. In this scheme parents are issued with vouchers or cheques spendable only on education at schools. There are several variants of the voucher scheme which have been well summarised by Maynard (1975) and Seldon (1986), but essentially the scheme is that all schools would be privatised and would charge fees, and the parents would pay these fees with their vouchers. It is argued that this would place consumer power in the hands of parents, foster competition between schools for the custom of parents, subject schools to the discipline of the market and raise schools' efficiency and standards.

While this proposal has been theoretically attractive to a number of economists, attempts to persuade politicians to introduce such a scheme have been disappointing. Even politicians sympathetic to this proposal, such as those in the Republican administrations in the United States and the Conservative administrations in Britain, have shied away from introducing any form of the voucher scheme. Probably the principal reason for the reluctance of sympathetic governments to introduce a voucher scheme lies in the massive reorganisation of the education system that would be required. This would entail the possible irruption of problems on an equally massive scale, such as some parents selling their vouchers, losing them, forging them and so forth, as well as possible further unforeseen difficulties. At all events, even governments in the United States and Britain strongly sympathetic to the free enterprise system have come to the conclusion that the voucher proposal is impractical. In Britain the Secretary of State for Education announced in 1983 that 'the voucher is dead'. Hence economists and other social scientists sympathetic to the privatisation of schools could usefully consider alternative ways of promoting a private sector in schools that would be more attractive to politicians.

It is here that the Japanese private senior high schools offer a useful alternative model for the privatisation of schools. The Japanese model suggests that a gradualist approach to the privatisation of schools would be a more feasible strategy. The Japanese experience shows that where private schools are subsidised by government to the extent of approximately 50 per cent of their cost, something like 40 to 50 per cent of parents in urban areas will opt for private education. The principal advantage of adopting the Japanese model in the West is that the gradualist nature of the strategy ensures that at no stage can massive problems arise to cause dislocation and political embarrassment. If the Japanese model were adopted, then from a certain date the government would introduce subsidies for private schools. These subsidies would be paid either on a straight *per capita* basis according to the number of children in the school, as in Japan, or on a varying basis according to parental income, as was the case for fee paying children at the former direct grant schools in Britain and in the present British assisted places scheme. Whichever form of subsidy were introduced, the only immediate effect would be that the school fees for parents would fall. This would produce an increase in demand for private education, and gradually private schools would expand and new private schools would be provided to meet this demand.

The attractiveness of such a gradualist strategy is that once a substantial number of subsidised private schools were established the private sector can be expected to grow in strength without further political attention. The critical proportion for private schools is probably around 20 per cent. At this proportion it would become politically impossible for governments hostile to private education to remove the subsidy, because the number of voters who would be alienated would be too great. Furthermore, once a private sector of around 20 per cent had been achieved, increasing affluence and the superior efficiency of private schools would ensure that they continued to grow in numbers.

Even without government subsidies the demand for private schools is sufficiently strong for new private schools to be established in Britain, such as the new private grammar school in Leicester, and in the United States, where the numbers of children in private schools increased by 60 per cent during the 1970s (Boyer, 1983). With government subsidies the growth of private schools would be much faster, and there is every reason to anticipate that before very long around half the children in urban areas in Western nations would be attending private schools, as is the case with the senior high schools in Japan. Although a gradualist strategy for the promotion of private schools would not achieve the total privatisation of education at a stroke that would be secured by the voucher scheme, it is far more likely to be attractive to politicians and therefore to be implemented. The Japanese experience shows that the achievement of a 40 to 50 per cent private school sector in urban areas is a perfectly feasible objective and the Japanese model is one that neo-liberals in the West would be wise to consider seriously.

8.8 CONCLUSIONS

This final chapter has been concerned with the lessons that can profitably be learned in the West from the high educational standards in Japan, and from the way in which these are achieved. It is proposed that four broad principles have emerged and they are summarised here.

(a) Financial Resources

Japanese educational standards are achieved without greater financial resources than those available to schools in the West. This is an important negative conclusion. Much of the efforts of governments in the West to raise educational standards has consisted of increasing public expenditure on education. Government expenditure on education has approximately doubled in real terms in Britain, the United States and much of Continental Europe in the decades since the end of World War Two. Yet there is little evidence to suggest that these increases have produced commensurate rises in educational standards, and in the United States there is clear evidence that educational standards have declined (Lerner, 1983). Comparisons between schools in the West have failed to show that greater expenditures are associated with higher standards. The Japanese experience of high educational standards, secured at only moderate cost, confirms the conclusion that educational standards do not respond so well as has been hoped to increasing financial resources. Western governments should look in other directions for ways to increase educational standards.

(b) Incentives for School Children

The Japanese experience suggests that the first principle for raising educational standards lies in the provision of incentives for school children to undertake academic work. The role of incentives in motivating work effort is well recognised in psychology and economics, but in education it has not received the attention it deserves. The most powerful incentives appear to be examinations, whose results school children perceive as important for their future careers. While many educationists have deprecated the use of examinations as motivators, and advocate instead the promotion of intrinsic motivation to acquire learning for its own sake, leading psychological theories of socialisation state that intrinsic motivation is developed as a consequence of experience of external incentives.

(c) Length of the School Year

The second principle to be derived from Japan is that an important determinant of educational standards is the length of the school year. Japanese children are in school approximately a third longer than their counterparts in Britain, the United States and much of Continental Europe, so that by mid-adolescence they have enjoyed the equivalent of some additional three years of education. It is remarkable how little consideration has been given in the West to the relatively short and wholly arbitrary school year, and to the possibility of lengthening it. No discussion of this factor will be found in standard textbooks on education, nor does it appear to have been given any thought by government ministers or their advisers. There is every reason to anticipate that a substantial lengthening of the school year would lead to an improvement of educational standards in the West among more able children. However, there must be some doubt about its advantageous effect among the less able. The efficiency of both teaching and learning would need to be improved before there could be any confident expectation that an increase in the length of the school year would have any useful results for children in the lower ability range.

(d) Incentives for Teachers

The third principle to be learned from Japanese education is the significance of incentives for teachers to work efficiently. These are weak in the West and much stronger in Japan. Although there has been some awareness in recent years in Britain and the United States of the weakness of incentives for teacher efficiency, and some attempts have been made to introduce incentives such as evaluation proce- dures, merit awards and so forth, little practical progress has been made in this direction. In Japan there are three powerful incentives for teacher efficiency, namely the detailed specification of the curriculum by the Ministry of Education, the competition between high schools for examination successes, and the large numbers of private schools which are subject to the discipline of the market. All of these methods of rendering teachers more accountable to the public deserve consideration in the West.

References

ADLER, A. (1932) *What Life Should Mean to You* (London: Allen & Unwin).

AIKEN, L. R. (1971) 'Intellectual Variables and Mathematics Achievement: Directions for Research', *Journal of School Psychology* 9, 201–12.

ATKINSON, J. W. and RAYNOR, J. D. (1978) *Personality, Motivation and Achievement* (Washington: Hemisphere Publishing).

ANDERSON, C. S. (1985) 'The Investigation of School Climate', in G. R. Austin and H. Garber (eds), *Research on Exemplary Schools* (New York: Academic Press).

BANDURA, A. (1982) 'Self-efficacy Mechanism in Human Agency', *American Psychologist* 37, 122–47.

BENTHAM, Jeremy (1789) *An Introduction to the Principles of Morals and Legislation*. Reprinted in *The Utilitarians* (New York: Doubleday).

BERLINER, D. C. (1985) 'Effective Classroom Teaching', in G. R. Austin and H. Garber (eds) *Research on Exemplary Schools* (New York: Academic Press).

BERLYNE, D. E. (1950) 'Novelty and Curiosity as Determinants of Exploratory Behaviour', *British Journal of Psychology* 41, 68–80.

BLAHA, J. and WALLBROWN, F. H. (1984) 'Hierarchical Analyses of the WISC and the WISC-R: Synthesis and Clinical Implications', *Journal of Clinical Psychology* 40, 557–71.

BONO, E. DE (1977) *Lateral Thinking* (Harmondsworth: Penguin Books).

BOYER, E. L. (1983) *High School: A Report on Secondary Education in America* (New York: Harper & Row).

BOYSON, R. (1972) *Education: Threatened Standards* (Enfield, Middlesex: Churchill Press).

BULLOCK, A. (1975) *A Language for Life* (London: HMSO).

BURT, C. L. (1949) 'The Structure of the Mind: A Review of the Results of Factor Analysis', *British Journal of Educational Psychology* 19, 100–11.

CARROLL, J. (1963) 'A Model for School Learning', *Teachers' College Record* 64, 723–33.

CATTELL, R. B. (1971) *Abilities: Their Structure, Growth and Action* (Boston: Houghton Mifflin).

CATTELL, R. B. (1979) *Personality and Learning Theory* (New York: Springer).

CATTELL, R. B., EBER, H. W. and TATSUOKA, M. M. (1970) *Handbook for the Sixteen Personality Factor Questionnaire* (Champaign, Illinois: Institute for Personality and Ability Testing).

CHARMS, R. DE (1968) *Personal Causation: The Internal Affective Determinants of Behaviour* (New York: Academic Press).

CHIPMAN, S. F., BRUSH, L. R. and WILSON, D. M. (1985) *Women and Mathematics* (Hillsdale, NJ: Lawrence Erlbaum).

CLARK, B. R. (1979) 'The Japanese System of Higher Education in

Comparative Perspective', in W. K. Cummings, I. Amano and K. Kitamura (eds) *Changes in the Japanese University* (New York: Praeger).

COCKCROFT, W. (1982) *Mathematics Counts* (London: HMSO).

COMBER, L. C. and KEEVES, J. (1973) *Science Achievement in Nineteen Countries* (New York: John Wiley).

COX, C. B. and BOYSON, R. (1977) *Black Paper* (London: Maurice Temple-Smith).

COX, C. B. and DYSON, A. F. (1969) *Black Paper One: Fight for Education* (London: Critical Quarterly Society).

CUMMINGS, W. K. (1980) *Education and Equality in Japan* (Princeton: Princeton University Press).

DARWIN, C. R. (1871) *The Descent of Man* (London: John Murray).

DECI, E. L. (1975) *Intrinsic Motivation* (New York: Plenum Press).

DENNISON, S. R. (1984) *Choice in Education* (London: Institute of Economic Affairs).

DOLLARD, J. and MILLER, N. E. (1950) *Personality and Psychotherapy* (New York: McGraw-Hill).

DONOVAN, J. D. and MADAUS, G. F. (1985) 'The Problems of Public Schools: The Catholic Connection', in G. R. Austin and H. Garber (eds) *Research on Exemplary Schools* (New York: Academic Press).

DURHAM, W. H. (1976) 'Resource Competition and Human Aggression. Part I: A Review of Primitive War', *Quarterly Review of Biology* 51, 385–415.

DWECK, C. S. and ELLIOT, E. S. (1983) 'Achievement Motivation', in P. H. Mussen (ed) *Handbook of Child Psychology* (New York: John Wiley).

EDUCATION COMMISSION OF THE STATES (1983) *Action for Excellence* (Denver: ECS).

EVERHART, R. B. (1982) *The Public School Monopoly* (San Francisco: Pacific Institute for Public Policy Research).

EYSENCK, H. J. (1979) *The Structure and Measurement of Intelligence* (Berlin: Springer-Verlag).

EYSENCK, H. J. and EYSENCK, M. W. (1985) *Personality and Individual Differences* (New York: Plenum Press).

FENNEMA, E. and SHERMAN, J. (1977) 'Sex-related Differences in Mathematics Achievement, Spatial Visualisation and Affective Factors', *American Educational Research Journal* 14, 51–71.

FENNEMA, E. and TARTRE, L. A. (1985) 'The Use of Spatial Visualisation in Mathematics by Girls and Boys', *Journal of Research in Mathematics Education* 16, 184–206.

FLYNN, J. R. (1984) 'The Mean IQ of Americans: Massive Gains 1932–78', *Psychological Bulletin* 95, 24–51.

FOGELMAN, K. (1983) *Growing Up in Great Britain* (London: Macmillan).

FRENCH, J. W. (1964) 'Comparative Prediction of High School Grades by Pure Factor Aptitude, Information and Personality Measurement', *Educational and Psychological Measurement* 24, 321–29.

FRIEDMAN, M. (1962) *Capitalism and Freedom* (Chicago: University of Chicago Press).

FURNHAM, A. (1984) 'The Protestant Work Ethic: A Review of the Psychological Literature', *European Journal of Social Psychology* 14, 87–104.

GARDEN, J. (1986) *The Second International Study of Achievement in Mathematics* (Unpublished).

GLASS, G. V. and SMITH, M. L. (1978) *Meta-analysis of Research on the Relationship of Class Size and Achievement* (San Francisco: Far West Laboratory for Educational Research and Development).

GRAY, J. and HANNON, V. (1986) 'HMI's Interpretations of Schools' Examination Results', *Journal of Educational Policy* 1, 23–33.

HARTER, S. (1981). 'A Model of Intrinsic Mastery Motivation in Children', in W. A. Collins (ed.) *Minnesota Symposium on Child Psychology* vol XIV (Hillsdale, N.J.: Erlbaum).

HARNETT, R. F. and FELDMESSER, R. A. (1980) 'College Admissions Testing and the Myth of Selectivity', *APHE Bulletin* 32, 3–6.

HAYES, C., ANDERSON, A. and FONDA, N. (1984) *Competence and Competition: Training and Education in the Federal Republic of Germany, the United States and Japan* (London: National Economic Development Office).

HAYES, L. A. (1976) 'The Use of Group Contingencies for Behavioural Control: A Review', *Psychological Bulletin* 83, 628–48.

HILGER, S. M. I., KLETT, W. G. and WATSON, C. G. (1976) 'Performance of Ainu and Japanese Six-year-olds on the Goodenough-Harris Drawing Test', *Perceptual and Motor Skills* 42, 435–38.

HOVLAND, C. I., LUMSDAINE, A. A. and SHEFFIELD, F. D. (1949) *Experiments on Mass Communication* (Princeton, NJ: Princeton University Press).

HUSEN, T. (1967) *International Study of Achievement in Mathematics: A Comparison of Twelve Countries* (New York: John Wiley).

ICHIKAWA, Shogo (1979) 'Finance of Higher Education', in W. K. Cummings, I. Amano and K. Kitamura (eds) *Changes in the Japanese University* (New York: Praeger).

IWAWAKI, S., EYSENCK, S. B. G. and EYSENCK, H. J. (1980) 'The Universality of Typology: A Comparison between English and Japanese School Children', *Journal of Social Psychology* 112, 3–9.

JENSEN, A. R. (1977) 'Cumulative Deficit in IQ of Blacks in the Rural South', *Developmental Psychology* 13, 184–91.

JENSEN, A. R. (1980) *Bias in Mental Testing* (London: Methuen).

JOHNSON, D. W. and JOHNSON, R. T. (1983) 'The Socialisation and Achievement Crisis: Are Co-operative Learning Experiences the Solution?', in L. Bickman (ed.) *Applied Social Psychology Annual* (Beverly Hills, CA: Sage Publications).

JOHNSON, D. W., MARUYAMA, G., JOHNSON, R., NELSON, D. and SKON, L. (1981) 'Effects of Co-operative, Competitive and Individualistic Goal Structures on Achievement: A Meta-analysis', *Psychological Bulletin* 89, 47–62.

KARWEIT, N. (1985) 'Should we Lengthen the School Term?', *Educational Researchers* 14, 9–15.

KASHIWAGI, K., AZUMA, H. and MIYAKE, K. (1982) 'Early Maternal Influences upon Later Cognitive Development among Japanese Children: A Follow-up Study', *Japanese Psychological Research* 24, 90–100.

KEITH, A. (1948) *A New Theory of Human Evolution* (London: Watts).

KELLY, A. B. (1980) 'The Meaning of Mixed Ability Teaching', in C. Sewell (ed.) *Mixed Ability Teaching* (Driffield, England: Nafferton Books).

KOHLBERG, L. (1981) *Essays in Moral Development* (New York: Harper & Row).

LATHAM, G. P. and YUKI, G. A. (1975) 'A Review of Research on the Application of Goal Setting in Organisations', *Academy of Management Journal* 18, 824–45.

LERNER, B. (1983) 'Test Scores as Measures of Human Capital and Forecasting Tools', in R. B. Cattell (ed.) *Intelligence and National Achievement* (Washington, D.C: Institute for the Study of Man).

LEWIN, K. (1935) *A Dynamic Theory of Personality* (New York: McGraw-Hill).

LOCKE, E. A. (1968) 'Toward a Theory of Task Motivation and Incentives', *Organisational Behaviour and Human Performance* 3, 157–89.

LOCKE, E. A., SHAW, K. N., SAARI, L. M. and LATHAM, G. P. (1981) 'Goal Setting and Task Performance: 1969–1980', *Psychological Bulletin* 90, 125–52.

LOPREATO, J. (1984) *Human Nature and Biocultural Evolution* (Boston: Allen & Unwin).

LYNN, R. (1977) 'The Intelligence of the Japanese', *Bulletin of British Psychological Society* 30, 69–72.

LYNN, R. (1978) 'Ethnic and Racial Differences in Intelligence: International Comparisons', in R. T. Osborne, C. E. Noble and N. Weyl (eds) *Human Variation* (New York: Academic Press).

LYNN, R. (1982a) 'IQ in Japan and the United States Shows a Growing Disparity', *Nature* 297, 222–23.

LYNN, R. (1982b) 'A School Leaving Certificate for All', in D. Anderson (ed.) *Educated for Employment* (London: Social Affairs Unit).

LYNN, R. (1982c) 'National Differences in Anxiety and Extraversion', in B. Maher and W. B. Maher (eds) *Progress in Experimental Personality Research*, Vol. XI (New York: Academic Press).

LYNN, R., HAMPSON, S. L. and MAGEE, M. (1983) 'Determinants of Educational Achievement at 16 Plus: Intelligence, Personality, Home Background and School', *Personality and Individual Differences* 4, 473–81.

LYNN, R. and HAMPSON, S. (1986a) 'Intellectual Abilities of Japanese Children: An Assessment of 2½–8½-Year-Olds Derived from the McCarthy Scales of Children's Abilities', *Intelligence* 10, 41–58.

LYNN, R. and HAMPSON, S. (1986b) 'The Structure of Japanese Abilities: An Analysis in Terms of the Hierarchical Model of Intelligence', *Current Psychological Research and Reviews* 4, 309–22.

LYNN, R. and HAMPSON, S. (1986c) 'Further Evidence on the Cognitive Abilities of the Japanese: Data from the WPPSI', *International Journal of Behavioural Development*.

LYNN, R. and HAMPSON, S. (1986d) 'The Rise of National Intelligence: Evidence from Britain, Japan and the United States', *Personality and Individual Differences* 7, 23–32.

LYNN, R. (1987) 'The Intelligence of the Mongoloids: A Psychometric, Evolutionary and Neurological Theory', *Personality and Individual Differences* (to appear), 8, 813–844.

McCLELLAND, D. C. (1961) *The Achieving Society* (New York: John Wiley).

McCLELLAND, D. C. (1985) *Human Motivation* (Glenview, Illinois: Scott, Foresman).

McPHERSON, A. and WILLMS, J. D. (1986) 'Certification, Class Conflict, Religion and Community', in A. C. Kerckhoff (ed.) *Research in Sociology of Education and Socialisation*, vol. VI (Greenwich, Connecticut: JAI Press).

MARKLUND, S. (1962) *Size and Homogeneity of Class as Related to Scholastic Achievement* (Stockholm: Almqvist & Wiksell).

MARKS, J. and POMIAN-SRZEDNICKI, M. (1985) *Standards in English Schools Second Report* (London: National Council for Educational Standards).

MARSLAND, D. (1981) 'Education – Vast Horizons, Meagre Visions', in D. Anderson (ed.) *Breaking the Spell of the Welfare State* (London: Social Affairs Unit).

MASTERS, J. C., FURMAN, W. and BARDEN, R. C. (1977) 'Effects of Achievement Standards, Tangible Rewards, and Self-Dispensed Achievement Evaluations on Children's Task Mastery', *Child Development* 48, 217–24.

MAYNARD, A. (1975) *Experiment with Choice in Education* (London: Institute of Economic Affairs).

MEAD, M. (1935) *Sex and Temperament* (New York: William Morrow).

MESSICK, S. and JUNGEBLUT, A. (1981) 'Time and Method in Coaching for the SAT', *Psychological Bulletin* 89, 191–216.

MICHAELS, J. W. (1977) 'Classroom Reward Structures and Academic Performance', *Review of Educational Research* 47, 87–98.

MISAWA, G., MOTEGI, M., FUJITA, K. and HATTORI, K. (1984) 'A Comparative Study of Intellectual Abilities of Japanese and American Children on the Columbia Mental Maturity Scale', *Personality and Individual Differences* 5, 173–82.

MOMBUSHO (1975) *Educational Standards in Japan* (Tokyo: Ministry of Education, Science and Culture).

MOMBUSHO (1980) *Education in Japan* (Tokyo: Ministry of Education, Science and Culture).

MORTON-WILLIAMS, R. and FINCH, S. (1968) *Young School Leavers* (London: HMSO).

MOTEGI, M. (1984) 'Standardisation of the WISC-R and WPPSI', *Journal of Psychometry* 20, 2–8.

OECD (1971) *Reviews of National Policies for Education – Japan* (Paris: OECD).

O'LEARY, K. D. and DRABMAN, R. (1971) 'Token Reinforcement Programs in the Classroom: A Review', *Psychological Bulletin* 75, 379–98.

PARKERSON, J. H., SCHILLER, D. P., LOMAX, R. G. and WALBERG, H. J. (1984) 'Exploring Causal Models of Educational Achievement', *Journal of Educational Psychology* 76, 638–46.

PASSOW, H. H., NOAH, H. J., ECKSTEIN, M. A. and MALLEA, J. R. (1976) *The National Case Study: An Empirical Comparative Study of Twenty One Educational Systems* (Stockholm: Almqvist & Wiksell).

PETERS, R. S. (1965) *Ethics and Education* (London: Allen & Unwin).

POINCARE, H. (1913) 'Mathematical Creation', in G. H. Halstead (trans.) *The Foundations of Science* (New York: Science Press).

PURKEY, S. C. and SMITH, M. S. (1985) 'Educational Policy and School Effectiveness', in G. R. Austin and H. Garber (eds) *Research on Exemplary Schools* (New York: Academic Press).

RACHLIN, H., BATTALIO, R., KAGEL, J. and GREEN, L. (1981) 'Maximization Theory in Behavioural Psychology', *Behavioural Brain Sciences* 4, 371–417.

ROHLEN, T. P. (1983) *Japan's High Schools* (Berkeley: University of California Press).

RUTTER, M., MAUGHAN, B., MORTIMORE, P., OUSTON, J. and SMITH, A. (1979) *Fifteen Thousand Hours: Secondary Schools and their Effects on Children* (Cambridge, Massachusetts: Harvard University Press).

SCHMIDT, F. L. and HUNTER, J. F. (1981) 'Employment Testing: Old Theories and New Research Findings', *American Psychologist* 36, 1128–2237.

SELDON, A. (1986) *The Riddle of the Voucher* (London: Institute of Economic Affairs).

SHERIF, M. and SHERIF, C. W. (1953) *Groups in Harmony and Tension* (New York: Harper & Row).

SHIMAHARA, N. K. (1979) *Adaptation and Education in Japan* (New York: Praeger).

SLAVIN, R. E. (1977) 'Classroom Reward Structure: An Analytic and Practical Review', *Review of Educational Research* 47, 633–50.

SPENCE, J. T. and HELMREICH, R. L. (1983) 'Achievement Related Motives and Behaviors', in J. T. Spence (ed.) *Achievement and Achievement Motives* (San Francisco: W. H. Freeman).

SPENCER, H. (1892) *Principles of Ethics* (London: John Murray).

STAATS, A. W., FINLEY, J., MINKE, K. A., WOLF, M. and BROOKS, C. (1964) 'A Reinforcer System and Experimental Procedure for the Laboratory Study of Reading Acquisition', *Child Development* 35, 209–31.

STAATS, A. W., STAATS, C. K., SCHUTZ, R. E. and WOLF, M. M. (1962) 'The Conditioning of Textual Responses Using "Extrinsic" Reinforcers', *Journal of Experimental Analysis of Behaviour* 5, 33–40.

STAW, B. M. (1977) 'Motivation in Organisations: Toward Synthesis and Redirection', in B. M. Staw (ed.) *New Directions in Organisational Behaviour* (Chicago: St Clair Press).

STEVENSON, H. W. (1983) *Mathematics Achievement of Chinese, Japanese and American Children* (Annual Report, Center for Advanced Study in Behavioural Sciences, California).

STEVENSON, H. W. and AZUMA, H. (1983) 'IQ in Japan and the United States'. *Nature* 306, 291–92.

STEVENSON, H. W., STIGLER, J. W., LEE, S., LUCKER, G. W., KITAMURA, S. and HSU, C. (1985) 'Cognitive Performance of Japanese, Chinese and American Children', *Child Development* 56, 718–34.

STEVENSON, H. W., STIGLER, J. W., LUCKER, G. W., LEE, S., HSU, C. and KITAMURA, S. (1982) 'Reading Disabilities: The Case of Chinese, Japanese and English', *Child Development* 53, 1164–1181.

STIGLER, J. W., LEE, S., LUCKER, G. W. and STEVENSON, H. W. (1982) 'Curriculum and Achievement in Mathematics: A Study of Elementary School Children in Japan, Taiwan and the United States', *Journal of Educational Psychology* 74, 315–22.

TANNER, G. R. (1977) 'Expectations of Japanese and American Parents and Teachers for the Adjustment and Achievement of Kindergarten Children', (PhD thesis, Michigan State University).

TODA, M., SHINOTSUKA, H., McCLINTOCK, C. G. and STECH, F. J. (1978) 'Development of Competitive Behaviour as a Function of Culture, Age and Social Comparison', *Journal of Personality and Social Psychology* 36, 825–39.

TOLMAN, E. C. (1932) *Purposive Behaviour in Animals and Men* (New York: Appleton-Century-Crofts).

TREVOR-ROPER, H. (1967) *Religion, the Reformation and Other Essays* (London: Macmillan).

TURNER, E. W. (1972) 'The Effect of Long Summer Holidays on Children's Literacy', *Educational Research* June, 182–86.

VAN LAWICK-GOODALL, J. (1967) 'Mother-Offspring Relationships in Free Ranging Chimpanzees', in D. Morris (ed.) *Primate Ethology* (London: Weidenfeld & Nicolson).

VERNON, P. E. (1950) *The Structure of Human Abilities* (London: Methuen).

VERNON, P. E. (1979) *Intelligence: Heredity and Environment* (San Francisco: W. H. Freeman).

VOGEL, E. F. (1979) *Japan as Number One* (Cambridge, Massachusetts: Harvard University Press).

VROOM, V. (1964) *Work and Motivation* (New York: John Wiley).

WALBERG, H. J. (1984) 'American Educational Productivity', *Educational Leadership*, May.

WALBERG, H. J., HARNISCH, D. L. and TSAI, S. (1985) *Mathematics Productivity in Japan and Illinois* (Unpublished).

WEBER, M. (1904) *The Protestant Ethic and the Spirit of Capitalism* trans, by T. Parsons. (New York: Charles Scribner's Sons).

WHITE, R. W. (1959) 'Motivation Reconsidered: The Concept of Competence', *Psychological Review* 66, 297–333.

WILSON, E. O. (1975) *Sociobiology: The New Synthesis* (Cambridge, Massachusetts: Harvard University Press).

WILSON, E. O. (1978) *On Human Nature* (Cambridge, Massachusetts: Harvard University Press).

WILSON, J. Q. and HERRNSTEIN, R. (1985) *Crime and Human Nature* (New York: Simon & Schuster).

WYNNE-EDWARDS, V. C. (1962) *Animal Dispersion in Relation to Social Behaviour* (Edinburgh: Oliver & Boyd).

ZANDER, A. (1971) *Motives and Goals in Groups* (New York: Academic Press).

ZANDER, A. (1980) 'The Origins and Consequences of Group Goals', in L. Festinger (ed.) *Retrospections on Social Psychology* (Oxford: Oxford University Press).

Name Index

Adler, A. 82
Aiken, L. R. 59
Atkinson, J. W. 81
Anderson, A. 48, 134
Anderson, C. S. 68
Azuma, H. 54, 58

Bandura, A. 68
Barden, R. C. 69
Battaglio, R. 62
Bentham, S. 61
Berliner, D. C. 68, 96, 132
Berlyne, D. E. 83
Blaha, J. 58
Bono, E. de 126
Boyer, E. L. 2, 141
Boyson, R. 1, 124
Brooks, C. 63
Brush, L. R. 59
Bullock, A. 1, 122, 134
Burt, C. L. 54

Callaghan, J. 1
Carroll, J. 112
Cattell, R. B. 53, 82
Charms, R. de 83
Chipman, S. F. 59
Clark, B. R. 44
Cockcroft, W. 1, 124, 134
Comber, L. C. 9, 10, 17, 84, 98,
    105, 111, 112, 117
Cox, C. B. 1, 124
Cummings, W. K. 64, 87, 95, 114

Darwin, C. R. 101
Deci, E. L. 83
Dennison, S. R. 139
Dollard, J. 84, 91
Donovan, J. D. 2
Drabman, R. 63, 70
Durham, W. H. 101
Dweck, C. S. 81
Dyson, A. F. 1

Eber, H. W. 82
Eckstein, M. A. 104, 106, 116
Elliot, E. S. 81
Everhart, R. B. 139
Eysenck, H. J. 52, 55, 84, 91, 125
Eysenck, M. W. 84, 91
Eysenck, S. B. G. 125

Feldmesser, R. A. 76
Fennema, E. 59
Finch, S. 73
Finley, J. 63
Flynn, J. R. 53
Fogelman, K. 111
Fonda, N. 48, 134
French, J. W. 59
Friedman, M. 139, 140
Fujita, K. 53
Furman, W. 69
Furnham, A. 81

Garden, J. 15
Glass, G. V. 111
Gray, J. 130
Green, L. 62

Hampson, S. L. 18, 52, 53, 55, 81,
    138
Hannon, V. 130
Harter, S. 83
Harnett, R. F. 76
Harnisch, D. L. 14, 118
Hattori, K. 53
Hayes, C. 63
Hayes, L. A. 48, 134
Helmreich, R. L. 81, 82
Herrnstein, R. 62
Hilger, S. M. L. 53
Hovland, C. I. 63
Hunter, J. F. 103
Husen, T. 4, 5, 7, 17, 85, 86, 95,
    98, 107, 108, 109, 111, 114, 115,
    126

Ichikawa, S. 44
Iwawaki, S. 125

Jensen, A. R. 17, 52, 55
Johnson, D. W. 63, 77
Johnson, R. T. 63, 77
Jungeblut, A. 76

Kagel, J. 62
Karweit, N. 114
Kashiwagi, K. 58
Keeves, J. 9, 10, 85, 98, 105, 111, 112, 117
Keith, A. 101
Kelly, A. B. 91
Klett, W. G. 53
Kohlberg, L. 84, 91

Latham, G. P. 68, 69
Lee, S. 11, 18, 58, 64, 95, 98, 117, 118
Lerner, B. 2, 124, 134, 142
Lewin, K. 68
Locke, E. A. 68, 69
Lomax, R. G. 3, 52, 61, 94, 112, 128
Lopreato, J. 82
Lucker, G. W. 11, 18, 58, 64, 95, 98, 117, 118
Lumsdaine, A. A. 63
Lynn, R. 18, 52, 53, 55, 56, 58, 74, 81, 125, 138

McClelland, D. C. 81, 84, 88, 91
McClintock, C. G. 87
McPherson, A. 30
Madaus, G. F. 2
Magee, M. 52, 81, 138
Mallea, J. R. 104, 106, 116
Marklund, S. 111
Marks, J. 30
Marsland, D. 139
Maruyama, G. 63, 77
Masters, J. C. 69
Maughan, B. 138
Maynard, A. 139, 140
Mead, M. 100
Messick, S. 76
Michaels, J. W. 63, 70, 71, 77, 100

Miller, N. E. 84, 91
Minke, K. A. 63
Misawa, G. 53
Miyake, K. 58
Mortimore, P. 138
Morton-Williams, R. 73
Motegi, M. 53, 54

Nelson, D. 63, 77
Noah, H. J. 104, 106, 116

O'Leary, K. D. 63, 70
Ouston, J. 138

Parkerson, J. H. 3, 52, 61, 94, 112, 128
Passow, H. H. 104, 106, 107, 114, 115, 116
Peters, R. S. 91
Poincaré, H. 126
Pomian-Srzednicki, M. 30
Purkey, S. C. 131, 132, 137

Rachlin, H. 62
Raynor, J. D. 81
Rohlen, T. P. 36, 46, 64, 94, 125
Rutter, M. 138

Saari, L. M. 68, 69
Schiller, D. P. 3, 52, 61, 94, 112, 128
Schmidt, F. L. 103
Schutz, R. E. 63
Seldon, A. 100, 139, 140
Shaw, K. N. 68, 69
Sheffield, F. D. 63
Sherif, C. W. 100
Sherif, M. 100
Sherman, J. 59
Shimahara, N. K. 26
Shinotsuka, H. 86
Skon, L. 63, 77
Slavin, R. E. 63, 77, 80, 100
Smith, A. 138
Smith, M. L. 111
Smith, M. S. 131, 132, 137
Spearman, C. 54, 55, 56, 57, 60
Spence, J. T. 81, 82
Spencer, H. 101

Staats, A. W.   63
Staats, C. K.   63
Staw, B. M.   62
Stech, F. J.   87
Stevenson, H. W.   11, 14, 18, 54,
  58, 64, 86, 88, 89, 95, 96, 98,
  117, 118, 128
Stigler, J. W.   11, 13, 17, 18, 58, 64,
  95, 98, 117, 118

Tanner, G. R.   18, 88
Tartre, L. A.   59
Tatsuoka, M. M.   82
Toda, M.   86
Tolman, E. C.   68
Trevor-Roper, H.   81
Turner, E. W.   128

Van Lawick-Goodall, J.   83
Vernon, P. E.   52, 54, 55
Vogel, E. F.   78
Vroom, V.   62

Walberg, H. J.   3, 14, 17, 52, 61,
  64, 94, 111, 112, 118, 128
Wallbrown, F. H.   58
Watson, C. G.   53
Weber, M.   80, 81, 84
White, R. W.   83
Willms, J. D.   30
Wilson, D. M.   59
Wilson, E. O.   82, 101
Wilson, J. Q.   62
Wolf, M.   63
Wynne-Edwards, V. C.   82

Zander, A.   101

Subject Index

Achievement
  in mathematics   4–9, 11–16, 17, 58, 59
  in reading   11–14, 58
  in science   9–11, 17, 127
Achievement motivation   81–2, 84, 92
American High School Mathematics Test   14
Attitudes to school work   85, 86
Anxiety   125
Australia   5, 7, 10, 98, 105, 106, 109, 112, 115

Belgium   5, 7, 10, 16, 86, 98, 104, 105, 106, 112, 115
Black Papers   1
Bullock Report   1, 122

Canada   16
Child-rearing practices   84
  and independence   84, 88
Chile   10
Class size   37, 110–12
  and educational attainment   110
Cockcroft Report   1
Competence motivation   83, 84
Competitiveness   82, 83, 84, 92, 100
  survival value   82, 86–87, 101
Competition   28, 29, 63, 76–9, 119
  and self-esteem   107
  between schools   99–102, 136–7
  and work effort   100
Comprehensivisation   33–9
Conditioning   83–5, 90
  and socialisation   84, 91
Conformity   126–7
Co-operation   76
Creativity   126–7
Cumulative advantage   16–17
Curiosity, survival value   83
Curriculum   9, 12, 18, 23, 26, 75, 76
  coverage of   98
  government specification of   96–9, 119, 129, 132–6

Demoralisation   127, 128
Discipline
  of the market   102, 140
  in schools   95–6
Dominance   82

Educational standards   128
  age trends in   16–17
  in Britain   1
  in Japan   2–3, 134
  and teaching   138
  in USA   2
Elite schools   19, 30, 31–2, 71–2
Engineering   127
England   5, 6, 7, 9, 10, 16, 98, 104, 105, 106, 109, 112, 115
Entrance examinations   23, 26, 27, 31, 37, 49, 65–6, 68–9, 71–2, 75–6, 78, 121
Evaluation of teachers   95
Examination hell   23, 65
Examinations, as credentials   123
Extrinsic motivation   61–79, 90–3
  and incentives   91

Fees   18, 19, 20, 23, 30, 40–1, 43–4, 87–8, 141
Financial resources of schools   108–9, 121
  and educational achievement   109, 142
Finland   7, 10, 16, 98, 105, 106, 109, 112, 115
France   5, 7, 8, 16, 48, 98, 105, 109, 112, 115

Germany (West)   5, 7, 8, 10, 48, 98, 104, 105, 106, 109, 112, 113, 115, 125
Goals   67–9, 74, 77
  challenging   69
  proximate sub-goals   68–9
  specific   67–8
Goal-setting   68

Graduate recruitment 46, 47, 49
Graduation diploma 74, 79
Greece 86

Head teachers 97, 131
Hedonic calculus 61
Hibiya 28, 31, 35
Homework 64, 86, 89, 94, 95–6
  in mathematics 115, 116, 117–18
Hong Kong 16
Hungary 10, 11, 16, 86, 87, 104,
    105, 106, 112, 115, 125

Illinois 14, 118
Illiteracy 124, 134
Imperial universities 43
Incentives 62, 68, 69, 99, 121–8
  and achievement 62–5, 121, 143
  and crime 62
  and examinations 73–4, 78,
    122–4
  grades 63, 70–1, 78
  for less able 127–8
  in Japanese education 65, 92
  marks and tokens 62, 63, 70–1,
    78
India 10
Instruction time 97, 113–19, 143
  and educational
    achievement 113, 117
  length of school day 115
  length of school year 114, 128–9
Intelligence 52–60
  age trends 57
  and educational achievement 52,
    58–60
  non-verbal 53, 54
  pattern of 58, 60
  rise in 53
  urban–rural differences 54
Intelligence tests
  Columbia Mental Maturity
    Scale 53
  McCarthy Scales of Children's
    Abilities 55
  non-verbal 52
  WISC–R 54, 55, 58
  WPPSI 55
International Study of Achievement

  in Mathematics 4–9, 15–16,
    98, 104, 107, 108, 111
International Study of Achievement
  in Science 9–11, 98, 104, 107,
    111
Intrinsic motivation 61, 80–90
  development of 83–5, 87–90
  in Japanese schoolchildren 85
IQ Box 18
Iran 10
Israel 5, 7, 98, 112, 115
Italy 10, 98, 104, 105, 106, 112, 115

Japan Scholarship Foundation 41
Japanese parents 49–50
Japanese press 27–8
Juku 23–6, 47, 102, 119
Junior high schools 22–3

Kindergarten 18–20
Kobe 34

Lifelong employment 66
Loans 41, 44
Luxembourg 16

Maladjustment 125
Market, discipline of 102, 140
Maximisation of utility 61
Merit awards 131–2
Minimum competence tests 75, 79,
  123–4
Ministry of Education 21, 25, 26,
  40, 41, 97, 129, 134
Minneapolis 11, 12, 14, 86, 88, 95,
  117, 128
Monopolies 139
Moral education 21–2, 134–5
Moral values 84
Motivation 29, 30, 47–9, 61, 68,
  100, 124
  and educational
    achievement 61–5
  of Japanese schoolchildren 64–5
Music 21

Nada 36, 38
National Assessment of Educational
  Progress 2

National Children's Bureau   110
Netherlands   5, 7, 8, 10, 16, 98, 104, 105, 106, 109, 112, 115
New Zealand   10, 16, 98, 105, 106, 112, 113, 115
Nishi   35
Nobel prizes   126

OECD   33

Power of exit   139
Primary schools   20–2, 55
Private schools   22, 30–6, 102–3
   and efficiency   102, 132, 138–40
Privatisation of schools   138–40
Protestant work ethic   80–1, 84, 92

Reinforcement   61, 63, 64, 69
Royal Commission on Technical Education   134

Scholastic Aptitude Test   2, 76, 78
School effectiveness   89, 137, 138
School leaving   23, 48, 64, 103, 124
School inspectors   130–1, 132
School year, length   114, 128–9
Scotland   5, 7, 10, 16, 98, 104, 105, 106, 109, 112, 115
Selection   71–3, 128
Self-esteem   101
Sendai   11, 12, 14, 86, 88, 95, 117, 128
Senior high schools   26–33, 65, 123, 140
Sex differences, in mathematics ability   59
Social class   20, 138
Social learning theory   100
Socialisation for achievement   89–90
Social mobility   39
Spatial ability
   and geometry   59
   of Japanese   54–7
Specialisation   6
Spearman's g   54, 55, 56, 57
   and educational achievement   60

State subsidies   39, 40, 141
Status hierarchy of schools   23, 26–8, 38, 44–5, 49, 66, 123
Student loans   41, 44
Suicide   125
Sweden   5, 7, 10, 16, 98, 104, 105, 106, 109, 111, 112, 115

Taiwan   11–13
Teachers
   ability   103–5
   accountability   132, 138
   efficiency   99, 124, 129–32, 137
   incentives   129–32
   merit awards   131–2
   professionalism   50, 94–6, 119, 135
   pupil ratios   111–12
   quality of instruction   94, 98
   salaries   40, 106–8
   training   105–6, 130
Technical colleges   41–2
Technical training   42, 134
Thailand   10
Tokyo   18, 25, 26, 30, 31, 34, 35

Umigaoka   34
United Nations Organisation   109, 110
United States   2, 5, 10, 16, 48, 98, 105, 106, 109, 111, 112, 115
United States Education Commission   122, 124
Universities   21, 26, 42–7
University of Tokyo   43, 45, 46, 47, 49
University schools   20

Values   50
Verbal ability   55, 56, 57, 58, 59
Visuospatial ability   55, 56, 57, 58, 59
Vocational high schools   41–2
Vouchers   140

Work motivation   91–2, 124
   and incentives   122–5